The HAPPINESS
Workbook

Hilary Pereira

Dedication

Writing a book on how to be happy has been a journey of enlightenment for me as much as it will be, I hope, for you the reader. Happiness is in many ways subjective, but I have tried to look at the subject as a whole in a more objective way and to provide exercises and insights that will help you to identify and shape the future of your own personal fulfilment and contentment. This book is dedicated to the memory of my parents, whose unfailing support and mentoring throughout the time I spent with them, in childhood and beyond, laid the foundations for my own personal happiness. It's also for my family and friends now, who enrich my life in so many ways it's impossible to count.

Hilary Pereira is a freelance writer and editor with special interest in health, lifestyle and parenting. During her 20-year career she has written extensively across the market, producing five books and publishing articles in the popular parenting press as well as national newspapers. Hilary is an experienced broadcaster and has appeared on TV news programmes as well as national and local radio stations talking about health and family-related issues. She lives with her family in Surrey.

The HAPPINESS Workbook

Hilary Pereira

Teach Yourself®

Hodder Education

338 Euston Road, London NW1 3BH.

Hodder Education is an Hachette UK company

First published in UK 2012 by Hodder Education

First published in US 2012 by The McGraw-Hill Companies, Inc

British Library Cataloguing in Publication Data: a catalogue record for this title is available from the British Library.

Library of Congress Catalog Card Number: on file

10 9 8 7 6 5 4 3 2 1

The publisher has used its best endeavours to ensure that any website addresses referred to in this book are correct and active at the time of going to press. However, the publisher and the author have no responsibility for the websites and can make no guarantee that a site will remain live or that the content will remain relevant, decent or appropriate.

The publisher has made every effort to mark as such all words which it believes to be trademarks. The publisher should also like to make it clear that the presence of a word in the book, whether marked or unmarked, in no way affects its legal status as a trademark.

Every reasonable effort has been made by the publisher to trace the copyright holders of material in this book. Any errors or omissions should be notified in writing to the publisher, who will endeavour to rectify the situation for any reprints and future editions.

Hachette UK's policy is to use papers that are natural, renewable and recyclable products and made from wood grown in sustainable forests. The logging and manufacturing processes are expected to conform to the environmental regulations of the country of origin.

www.hoddereducation.co.uk

Cover image © Anterovium - Fotolia

Typeset by Cenveo Publisher Services.

Printed in Great Britain by CPI Group (UK) Ltd, Croydon, CR0 4YY

Acknowledgements

I'd like to thank family, friends, philosophers and psychologists who have all contributed to the book. I'd also like to thank my publisher, Sam Richardson, for giving me the opportunity to write the book, and the whole team at Hodder Education whose hard work has helped bring the project to fruition.

Contents

Introduction

→ **Happiness is for everyone**

'When I was in grade school, they told me to write down what I wanted to be when I grew up.

I wrote down happy. They told me I didn't understand the assignment. I told them they didn't understand life.'

John Lennon, singer and songwriter

In my career as a journalist, author and, more recently, as a Member of the Guild of Health Writers, I have had the opportunity to research and write about a wide variety of subjects with input from psychologists, life coaches and many other health and wellbeing experts. I was involved for many years in the parenting sector and am a former Deputy Editor of *Mother & Baby* magazine. After having my own daughter, I expanded my writing to focus more and more on health and lifestyle. All of these different aspects of life inevitably contribute to our day-to-day wellbeing. Equally, they can contribute to unhappiness and a lack of personal fulfilment. I have learnt a lot whilst researching and writing about what happiness can mean and how it is within everyone's power to find greater peace and contentment. Happiness is for everyone, but it doesn't just happen. We need the ability to stand back and examine ourselves objectively, and we also need the right tools with which to effect some changes in order to find our inner happiness and apply it to our daily lives. This book is your happiness toolkit.

→ Happiness as a subject

The concept of happiness is somewhat abstract and subjective. It means different things to different people: for some it's financial security; for others it's parenthood, family or career progression, personal relationships, fulfilment or good health; for most of us it's a combination of all of these things. *The Happiness Workbook* takes an objective look at the many influences that affect how contented we are, such as our own experiences of childhood and growing up; our history of acceptance or rejection; our personal circumstances and how well we are able to measure and cope with our own successes and failures. I have looked at the concept from lots of different viewpoints and included reflections, food for thought and practical exercises to enable you to discover what is holding you back from greater happiness and how you can bring it into your life by making a few adjustments – some simple and instantly achievable, others aimed at making longer term changes. The book doesn't offer formal therapy but draws on my own research as well as the extensive advice and insight shared with me by the experts I have had the pleasure and privilege of working with during my writing career. I hope it will be a useful companion to anyone looking towards a happier and more fulfilling future.

How to use this workbook

'If you want to live a happy life, tie it to a goal, not to people or things.'

Albert Einstein,
physicist and philosopher of science

The *Teach Yourself* series of workbooks is intended ultimately to empower the reader to achieve a skill, ambition or dream through enlightenment, empowerment and practical exercises. In *The Happiness Workbook*, we'll first establish how happy or otherwise you are right now, then we'll go through the book chapter by chapter, working together to explore what happiness means to you; what is getting in the way of your personal happiness and how best to achieve greater fulfilment and contentment. Some sections are aimed at people who are in a relationship; some include advice for parents; there are also references to singledom. In lots of cases, the exercises can be useful even where the chapter content doesn't wholly apply to your personal circumstances.

The book is constructed as a series of short discussions and self-evaluations, punctuated throughout with practical exercises you'll complete on your journey through the chapters. You'll also find within the pages lots of quotes from eminent people which I hope will uplift and inspire you. At the end of the book you'll be asked to re-evaluate how happy you are compared with the beginning of the process. The aim is that you'll be in a position to see how much your self-esteem and general happiness levels have increased, and that you'll have adopted a new mindset and way of life that will enable you to feel more optimistic about the future.

In Chapter 1 we'll first of all evaluate just how happy you judge yourself to be now and what you believe happiness means to you. We'll go on to examine:

▶ the differences between fleeting moments of elation, short but significant periods of happiness and longer term contentment and fulfilment;
▶ how your upbringing and childhood experiences may have influenced your self-esteem and general disposition in adulthood;
▶ how to move past negative beliefs ingrained from childhood;
▶ how to recognize if you may be suffering from depression.

Chapter 2 requires a degree of introspection and self-analysis. You'll discover how you regard yourself and why – and you'll be challenged on some of the more negative aspects of your self-image and encouraged to turn some of your more entrenched thinking on its head. We'll also look at:

▶ the importance of self-acceptance and how to achieve this, even if your opinion of yourself is quite low right now;
▶ how to set goals to improve your levels of self-esteem;
▶ how well you look after yourself, physically and emotionally.

In Chapter 3 you'll have a chance to put all of your significant relationships, past and present, under the spotlight and work out what positive and negative influences each one has had on your current state of being. You may find a pattern emerging through failed relationships, and you'll be guided in how to draw on some of the more positive aspects when planning your future happiness. You'll discover:

▶ the importance of praise and the emotional impact of criticism, especially when the latter outweighs the former;

▶ tips for recreating the early closeness of your relationship and working together to find a new equilibrium and sense of belonging.

Chapter 4 examines that inner voice we all have which can by turns empower us, placate us, counsel us or drag us down. You'll practise listening to the tone of your inner voice and either accepting it or challenging it until it becomes a force for good in your life. You'll find out:

▶ how to step away from yourself and look at your life choices and your attitudes more objectively and impassively;

▶ the importance of giving yourself permission to indulge yourself;

▶ how to regard life's mistakes as important reminders that we are all fallible, and that every slip-up is in itself a lesson to value and take forward;

▶ how you can laugh yourself happy even when you're not. (Yes, really!)

In Chapter 5, we'll be taking a close look at your family dynamics, examining your relationships with your parents, your siblings and your own children, and how they interface in both positive and negative ways. We'll look at:

▶ the value of keeping parental boundaries in your relationships with your kids, even if you genuinely feel as if you're best friends;

▶ how drawing a line in the sand can boost your feelings of self-esteem;

▶ how boundaries will engender a greater sense of security in your children.

Chapter 6 takes a look at your friendships and their impact on your happiness. Some of us subconsciously seek out people we perceive as being in some way 'weaker' than we are because this boosts our self-esteem; some of us do the reverse and align ourselves with people we secretly think are too good for us, because their acceptance of us makes us feel better about ourselves. Sometimes we hang on to friendships that are no longer fulfilling out of a sense of responsibility and guilt; at other times we let good people go by destroying the relationship with negativity. There's a chance to:

▶ examine what different friendships have meant to you at different periods in your life;
▶ learn how to recapture some of the happiness of the past and sift out the negative;
▶ discover how to build new friendships – perhaps via avenues you wouldn't normally consider.

In Chapter 7, the focus is on the importance in your life of materialism and financial security. This can mean vastly different things to different people, with some getting by happily on very little and others feeling threatened if they don't have enough back-up to deal with any financial eventuality. You'll have the opportunity to:

▶ reassess your own relationship with money and material possessions;
▶ discover and work on your personal spending/saving style;
▶ rethink your attitudes to personal wealth;
▶ learn that less can be more on the road to achieving personal happiness.

Chapter 8 examines lifestyle and whether yours is currently fulfilling or frustrating you. We'll look back at all the different phases in your life and what has changed along the way, for better or worse. You'll be encouraged to:

► make a life map to help you to analyse your personal journey;

► re-evaluate your current situation if it's contributing to your unhappiness;

► discover whether or not your general disposition is, in part, genetically imprinted;

► learn how to gain other people's acceptance of you as you are.

Chapter 9 takes a look at your sense of personal identity, which can become blurred or erased during the course of life and all its many changes. You'll:

► analyse which identity you've most enjoyed and why;

► look at ways of rediscovering parts of you that may have been long lost or forgotten;

► discover how to spend more time being the person you most enjoy being;

► learn how to value yourself as an individual, as well as in all the other roles you juggle daily;

► learn how to plan to make changes, whether short-term or in the future: and how sometimes just planning determinedly for change can lift your spirits until the time comes for implementation.

In Chapter 10, you'll discover that there are many different ways in which we can be spiritual, whether or not we have any religious faith. You'll teach yourself to:

► open your mind to wider possibilities;

► explore different spiritual practices and raise your EQ ('emotional quotient', also known as 'emotional intelligence');

► examine how giving more freely of yourself, both in charitable terms and in terms of time and love, can bring tremendous happiness and feelings of fulfilment.

In Chapter 11, we'll come to the end of our journey together, although you'll always have the book to re-read and the exercises to revisit when you feel in need of some guided uplifting of the spirits. You'll:

▶ have another opportunity to evaluate your overall happiness levels – which hopefully will have improved markedly since Chapter 1;
▶ be given exercises to practise regularly, but with varying frequency, in order to keep you on the path to greater contentment, self-esteem and, in turn, happiness.

Ready? Let's go.

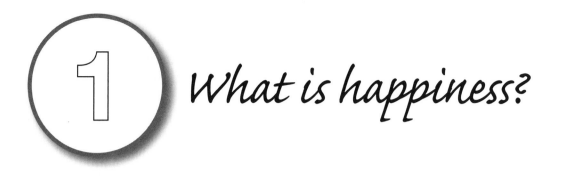

What is happiness?

'*You will never be happier than you expect. To change your happiness, change your expectation.*'

Bette Davis, Hollywood actress

Happiness has become a matter of national importance as evidenced by the current UK government conducting regular polls to ascertain levels of contentment of the nation, both as individuals and as a whole. The results are regarded as an important measure of its own success in introducing new policies and reshaping old thinking. 'Happiness economics' has become a term that's widely bandied around by politicians and the media.

So what is happiness? It's a term with many definitions, and one that means different things to different people. Some schools of thought maintain that it's a self-generated judgement of our personal situation at any given point in time; others say it's an ongoing state of mind. Ask around any group of friends and each will have different criteria for happiness – 'A bottle of wine on a Friday night'; 'A meal out with my other half'; 'Watching our children playing nicely together'; 'Passing a job interview' – but what makes us happy in the moment doesn't necessarily equate to true, ongoing, core happiness.

Some people equate ongoing happiness with excitement, passion, adventure and challenge; for others it's inner peace, self-awareness, self-acceptance and personal fulfilment. Some parents assert that they were never truly happy until they had their children – yet there can't be a parent in the world who hasn't experienced the resulting worry, anxiety, frustration, anger and panic which inevitably accompanies parenthood, and there must be many, too, who look back with some fondness at the relative freedom of their youth.

So is happiness defined by intermittent periods of pleasure or a continuing sense of wellbeing and satisfaction with our lot? The answer, again, will be different for different people. The aim of this book is to raise your awareness of what really makes *you* happy as an individual; to give you the tools to see the positive in challenging situations and to raise your overall, ongoing levels of happiness and self-esteem through self-analysis and a series of enlightening mental and practical exercises.

Of course, it would be completely unrealistic to expect to exist in a permanent state of ecstasy or even uninterrupted contentment, and it's arguable that in order to appreciate what real happiness is, we first have to have experienced sadness by way of contrast. Every human being will undergo periods of unhappiness or discontentment, whether through bereavement, lack of self-fulfilment, illness or any other unfortunate circumstance, but it's how we react to these experiences that will dictate to what extent we can find happiness afterwards. Some people fall into a decline or adopt a pessimistic view of the world as a whole after a misfortune; others pick themselves up and resolve to look for happier times ahead. Which of these two broad character types do you fit more closely?

Probably the best starting point when measuring whether we see ourselves as essentially happy or unhappy is to make an honest assessment of what proportion of our time and our lives overall is marked by contentment and pleasure as opposed to stress and sadness. Let's start by making just such an assessment with the first exercise of the book. We'll be revisiting this questionnaire at the end of the final chapter so you can re-evaluate your happiness level then.

SELF-EVALUATION QUESTIONNAIRE: HOW HAPPY ARE YOU RIGHT NOW?

Give each statement that's relevant to you a rating between 0–10, with 0 representing 'I completely disagree' and 10 representing 'I'm in total agreement'. Leave any statements that don't apply blank.

- ▶ I feel generally happy with my lot — 1
- ▶ I make the most of every day — 0
- ▶ I find enough time just for me — 10
- ▶ I am fulfilled in my work — 2
- ▶ I feel appreciated in my work — 8
- ▶ My relationship is working well — 0
- ▶ I feel I'm a good enough partner — 5
- ▶ I find parenthood fulfilling and rewarding most of the time — NO
- ▶ I feel I'm a good enough parent — 0
- ▶ I have high self-esteem — 2
- ▶ Overall, I think I'm an optimist — 2
- ▶ I expect good things to happen to me — 8
- ▶ Good things usually do happen to me — 6
- ▶ I feel loved and supported by my family — 10
- ▶ I laugh often — 8
- ▶ I have two or more close friends I can confide in — 2
- ▶ I feel that people respect me — 5
- ▶ I am spiritually fulfilled — 8
- ▶ I like who I am — 3
- ▶ I love my life! — 2

Total score — 109

Average score — 5.45

(Divide total score by number of questions answered.)

Add up your overall score, and then find your average mark out of ten by dividing this total by the number of questions you answered. This will give you your current overall happiness rating. If your average is seven or above, you're already doing quite well in the happiness stakes, although the fact that you're reading this book suggests that you may not have been completely honest with yourself. Any score of six or below shows that you have scope to improve your happiness levels – and you've come to the right place!

→ Is happiness laid down in childhood?

'The childhood shows the man, as morning shows the day.'

John Milton, English poet

Do happy children make happier adults? And are adults whose childhoods were less than charmed more likely to be discontented with their lot and to struggle to find personal fulfilment? Historically, psychoanalysts such as Sigmund Freud – and others who have followed him, including Polish psychologist Alice Miller – have expounded the theory that our individual experiences of childhood have a key significance in how we turn out as adults. The complexities of the relationships that are formed in childhood – specifically with our parents and through the subconscious mind – have long been considered instrumental in the formation of our adult minds. Freud was particularly interested in the theory that lost memory from infancy and early childhood could hold the key to our psychological wellbeing as adults, which is why he was an advocate of regression therapy, where adults are taken back under hypnosis to these very early stages and encouraged to recall long-repressed but significant memories. Whether or not we adhere to these theories, it's nevertheless a good point, now that we've established current levels of happiness, to look back at the influence our early lives might have had.

If you had an unsupportive or lonely childhood, you may have ingrained beliefs about yourself and your potential. But beliefs are only opinions, not facts, and they can be changed. Even if your childhood was, to the best of your recollection, a happy one, it doesn't follow that the values that were instilled in you as a child match the values you hold dear today. The idea is to hold on to any positive values from childhood that are still significant and important to you now, and to disregard anything that isn't helpful in influencing who you are today. As an adult, you are solely responsible for your own happiness, and you are also solely responsible and accountable for the values you choose to uphold. Improving your self-esteem will impact not only on your life, but on the lives of others around you, as it's only once we feel good about ourselves and don't need the approval of others in order to do so that we can be truly generous and kind to the people around us without any ulterior motive.

Exercise 1

OBJECTIVE REFLECTION

→ Think about your upbringing. Would you say your parents adopted a positive or negative approach to parenting?

I would say a bit of both, my parents were supportive but lay on the guilt quick

→ How did you learn to respond to any praise from your parents? Do you mirror either of your parents' own typical responses?

I would just say thank you, but no positive achievents weren't always praised

→ How about your response to criticism? Do you mirror either of your parents' own typical responses?

I shut down, I do not know how to take criticism

→ What are your earliest memories of reward, whether from parents, teachers or others? How do you feel about them now?

I remember _____ the _____ me
_____ stuffed bear one _____ _____

→ What are your earliest memories of punishment, whether from parents, teachers or others? How do you feel about them now?

➜ As a child, did you feel 'good enough'?

_____

_____

_____

➜ How was your self-esteem either built or undermined
and by whom?

_____

_____

_____

The exercise encourages you to think about things you may
have accepted before without questioning them, and to
re-evaluate these issues now from your adult perspective. If
you can see that your self-esteem was undermined by one
or both of your parents or another significant individual, it's
important to acknowledge and understand that this *was* not
and *is* not your fault. You can move forward from feelings of
inadequacy by evaluating your life now, which we'll be doing
together throughout the book. If you were over-praised by
your parent or parents, this can also have had a long-term
negative effect because sometimes when we're praised too
much or too often, we are set a precedent that unless we
maintain the same level of achievement which earned us that
praise, we'll be failing in some way. The lesson here is that
individual incidences of praise need to be valued individually.
Allowing ourselves to fail from time to time – or to fall short
of giving of our absolute best at all times – permits us to
feel that we are generally doing well enough. This allows the
praise we do receive to have a positive, if transient impact,
rather than making us feel pressure to 'keep up the good
work' without letting standards slide.

→ How our experiences translate to adulthood

'What is an adult? A child blown up by age.'

Simone de Beauvoir, French author and philosopher

A happy childhood doesn't guarantee a happy adulthood, although admittedly it's a good starting point. Those of us who were raised in a household that focused on fun as well as discipline, laughter as well as quiet reflection and celebration as well as responsibility will – as long as all other aspects of the family were more or less balanced – have had good foundations laid down, but these aren't impervious to outside influences. Sometimes, for instance, being with a negative or unconfident person long term can bring the sunniest of people down. Partners with very low self-esteem, for instance, can gradually grind through their other halves' layers of self-confidence and assuredness and set about destroying all that's positive about their characters. It's often done subconsciously, but the effect is that it allows the weaker partner to gain in power and undermine the previously happier person. The key to surviving such a relationship is either to acknowledge what's going on and why – and hopefully to get the weaker partner to seek counselling; or to leave the relationship and begin to rebuild your own confidence and happiness stores. In other cases, lots of sadness, loss or lack of success in adulthood can eventually destroy those happy foundations laid down in childhood. These can be rebuilt with a conscious effort, when you have the know-how.

An unhappy childhood is likely to have impacted negatively on your self-esteem as an adult. Feeling unloved or under-appreciated can lead to feelings of worthlessness, which in turn can give rise to loneliness and isolation. Abuse, whether physical, mental or sexual, is extremely damaging and needs careful resolution through professional counselling. Nevertheless, feelings of low self-worth can be very deeply ingrained and cause untold unhappiness.

In less extreme circumstances, labels we're given as children can perpetuate into adulthood, defining us in ways that are unjustified. Being told repeatedly 'You're very naughty', for example, can not only result in more of the apparently expected bad behaviour, but the label can carry over into adulthood, so that the affected now grown-up child harbours a deep-seated conviction that it's their destiny to be badly behaved or viewed as somehow disruptive or irksome. Similarly, if a child is over-praised (a subject we'll be examining in more detail later), they can grow into an over-confident adult with very high expectations. None of this is the fault of the child, but of the adults responsible for their upbringing. However, in adulthood, it's time for us all to re-examine why we are as we are, and whether perhaps it's time for change.

→ Moving past ingrained negative beliefs about ourselves from childhood

'It's never too late to have a happy childhood.'

Berkeley Breathed, children's book author/illustrator

Once you've accepted that the responsibility for whether or not your childhood was happy has to be taken, by and large, by your parents and other influential adults, you can start to look at things from a new, more adult perspective. It's not easy – especially in the case of an unhappy childhood – to adjust the way we think about things so that they become more relevant for who we are today, but it's nevertheless crucial to being able to move on and take responsibility for our own current and future happiness. Not to do so would be to remain in a childlike state – and that's not healthy for any grown-up, or for our relationships with other people.

Exercise 2

REVERSE THINKING

By deliberately reversing some of the ingrained negative ideas we have about ourselves, we can begin to feel more positive about both the past and the future.

▶ **Old thinking:** My parents didn't seem to love me much.

New thinking: I am loved and appreciated by people whose opinions I value today.

▶ **Old thinking:** I was treated unfairly as a child.

New thinking: I have every right to expect and receive fair treatment as an adult.

▶ **Old thinking:** I was horribly bullied at school.

New thinking: The experience of being bullied has given me greater empathy with others who suffer discrimination.

▶ **Old thinking:** I could have done better academically.

New thinking: I have many positive attributes that are nothing to do with exam results.

▶ **Old thinking:** I don't really deserve to be happy.

New thinking: Everyone, including me, has a perfect right to happiness.

▶ **Old thinking:** Happiness is unattainable for me.

New thinking: Happiness is a state of mind that I can generate from within myself.

It can be helpful to read through this exercise each morning and to repeat the new ways of thinking as positive mantras to set you up for the day ahead. Eventually they should become ingrained in your psyche so that your expectations are more realistic than before.

Now, on the next page, list down all the values from childhood that still matter to you now. Perhaps you were brought up in a faith to which you still remain true; maybe your parents' views on discipline had a positive influence on your own (whether or not you chose to follow or reject them); hopefully you were brought up to respect others' opinions as well as your own. There may be negative values that it's time to put behind you, too. Perhaps your parents looked down on those whose intellectual or material achievements didn't match their own; perhaps there was a tendency towards bigotry; maybe your input as a child was undervalued and you still feel you have nothing to contribute in terms of opinion or conversation. Refer to this list whenever you are questioning your new adult thinking or values.

CHILDHOOD VALUES THAT STILL MATTER TODAY

→ Recognizing our own achievements and abilities

'It is not the mountain we conquer, but ourselves.'

Sir Edmund Hillary, explorer

Achievements don't have to be remarkable to be worth remembering. When we look back at our achievements, however small or great, they can have the cumulative effect of making us feel generally happy with ourselves. Achievement suggests a level of effort that supersedes ability: ability isn't the same as achievement, it can come naturally or can be acquired and is always to be celebrated, but we deserve an extra pat on the back for those areas of ability we have gained through hard work, commitment and self-improvement. Every new ability, whatever the scale, is cause for celebration, whether it's baking a perfect sponge cake, managing on a budget, mastering a musical instrument or becoming a marathon runner!

Exercise 3

MY TOP TEN PROUDEST ACHIEVEMENTS

Take your time to think back through your life and remember as many achievements as possible. Perhaps you won a school prize or overcame a fear or phobia? Maybe you got a job offer against the odds or helped run a fundraising event? Have you been a school helper or championed a local charity? Think laterally, too. Perhaps your input has helped someone else to achieve? Have you bounced back from an unfortunate incident or time period? Jot them all down then list them in the chart provided. Feel the pride!

Age/life stage	Achievement
1	
2	
3	
4	
5	
6	
7	
8	
9	
10	

→ There's no happiness without sadness

'Behind every beautiful thing, there's some kind of pain.'

Bob Dylan, musician

In order to appreciate what true happiness is we all have to experience the reverse. Just as experiencing sleep deprivation, for example, allows us to appreciate one unbroken night's sleep, experiencing unhappiness makes the feeling of happiness more recognizable and valuable when it comes. So a degree of unhappiness does have a valuable place within our lives, hard as it may be to appreciate it while it's happening. None of us can tolerate an imbalance of sadness over happiness, however, and unnecessary sadness can be avoided if we make some subtle adjustments to the way we respond to uncomfortable or otherwise difficult situations.

Exercise 4

EMOTIONAL RESPONSE QUIZ

In each case, choose the answer that most closely represents your responses.

1 You get on with most of your colleagues, but try as you might you can't seem to win over one particular person. How do you feel?

 a. I feel unpopular, unlikeable and inadequate.

 b. I focus more on the fact that one person doesn't like me than that the others do.

c. It's great to get on well with some of the group, but my personal happiness isn't dependent on being universally liked.

2 You read three news reports in a week about knife crime involving young people. What impact does this have on you?

a. I feel depressed at the thought that our society is failing so badly.

b. I feel sorry for the victims but don't dwell on the news.

c. I feel moved to join a local campaign to end knife crime.

3 Your former best friend appears to have dropped you for no reason you can pinpoint. Who's to blame?

a. I am. If I was good enough company they'd still be calling me.

b. They are. They're being selfish and not thinking about how this is making me feel.

c. Probably no one. Sometimes friendships change direction for a while, but the rift is probably temporary.

4 A rowdy youth on the street criticizes your appearance. How does this make you feel?

a. They're right. I don't make enough of an effort and am unattractive to everyone.

b. I feel hurt and embarrassed, but a stranger's opinion shouldn't matter to me.

c. They are ignorant and socially inept; I, on the other hand, am neither.

5 You leave a phone message for your partner but they don't return your call. What do you think?

a. Our relationship is breaking down.

b. Perhaps I've done something to cause offence.

c. Clearly they're busy or haven't received the message.

If your answers are mostly 'a', you have issues with low self-esteem and tend to take a rather pessimistic view of life. This will be dealt with later in the book. Mostly 'b' answers show that you tend to take the middle ground and, whilst you're a bit sceptical, you can also see the other side. If you answered mostly 'c', you're able to look on the positive side and are generally optimistic. One of the aims of the book is to raise your levels of optimism generally. Pessimists tend to generate their own unhappiness, and it can have a knock-on effect: other people will inevitably prefer to spend more time around individuals with a sunnier outlook, and may grow tired of people who spend too much time thinking the worst.

Read over the 'c' answers and see if these could perhaps apply in your situation after all. This will in any case help you to adjust your thinking so that you can begin to learn how to seek the positive over the negative. Studies show that positive thinking alone can trigger more positive outcomes, so you may even be able to influence your own situation by altering your way of approaching a problem.

→ Mind over matter

'Most folks are about as happy as they make up their minds to be.'

Abraham Lincoln, 16th president of the USA

'It is not things in themselves that trouble us but our opinion of things.'

Epictetus, Greek philosopher

'There is nothing good or bad, but thinking makes it so.'

From William Shakespeare's *Hamlet*

The power of the mind is not be underestimated, as these three quotations illustrate. Many research studies have proven that our personal state of mind can have physiological effects. A science called 'neuroplasticity' studies the brain's ability to reorganize itself by forming new neural connections (pertaining to the nervous system), and this practice has helped people not only to adjust their perceptions of their own personal circumstances, but has even promoted healing after serious injury or disease. It's long been understood that stressful thinking can raise the blood pressure and cause muscle tension; dwelling on unhappy thoughts or images can sap the energy and even trigger depression. In the same way, positive thinking induces feelings of wellbeing and relaxation, and can reduce symptoms of stress. Some nervous or shy people have taught themselves to feel more confident by putting on a confident façade. Similarly, by presenting ourselves as happy, even if we're not genuinely feeling so, we can actually become happier.

Advocates of positive thinking believe that it's possible to make conscious decisions about how we regard life's events, and that with practice we can choose to see the positive in given situations. So, for example, instead of thinking 'The train is cancelled again and I'll be late for that meeting', we could think 'As long as I phone ahead, the meeting can be rescheduled and I'll have even more time to prepare'.

Exercise 5

THE POWER OF MEMORY

Meditating on happy events, relationships or periods in your life can reawaken a sense of happiness that you can enjoy again now. Compile a photo album of happy times and events. What made them especially happy? Can you recapture some of that happiness by mentally reliving these occasions? You can do this by setting aside 10–20 minutes of quiet time when you won't be interrupted, sitting with your eyes closed and bringing images of an occasion into your mind. As other thoughts occur to you, acknowledge them but let them go so that in the end you're focusing only on the feelings; physical sensations like smell, sound and taste; emotions; weather conditions; faces; dialogue and other aspects of the setting of your chosen memory. Really feel yourself being back in that setting and enjoy the sensations. When you've finished meditating, think whether you could create similar happy events. Check your diary or calendar and plan at least two events for the coming months that you can look forward to. They could include a family dinner; a picnic with friends; a school reunion; a weekend away or a special evening to be spent alone with your partner – or anything else you know you would enjoy that's not too costly or stressful to organize.

→ Recognizing depression

There's a difference between unhappiness and clinical depression, and whilst this book may help to lift your spirits in some ways, if you are truly depressed you must seek help from a doctor. Depression is most effectively treated if approached early on in the illness, when talking therapies and/or medication can help to halt its progress and start you on the road to recovery. The following can be signs of depression:

- ▶ feeling down more often than not
- ▶ feeling worse as the day wears on
- ▶ feeling weepy or crying for no apparent reason
- ▶ having difficulty sleeping at night
- ▶ wanting to sleep during the day
- ▶ loss of appetite
- ▶ loss of libido (sex drive)
- ▶ excessive tiredness
- ▶ inability to concentrate
- ▶ lack of interest in previously enjoyable things
- ▶ feelings of hopelessness
- ▶ feelings of worthlessness
- ▶ irritability
- ▶ indecisiveness
- ▶ suicidal feelings

If you are experiencing these symptoms in a way that's unusual for you, or in combination, seek advice from your GP or an online support group (see 'Taking it further' at the end of the book). There isn't the stigma attached to depression that there used to be when it was a less understood condition. It's important to get help, as this is an illness that can spiral downwards if allowed to go unchecked. The sooner treatment starts, the quicker your recovery is likely to be.

→ Happiness from loneliness

'At the innermost core of all loneliness is a deep and powerful yearning for union with one's lost self.'

Brendan Francis Behan, Irish playwright

Focusing on what makes you feel happy – and perhaps seeking out groups of like-minded individuals – can help to overcome loneliness, which for some people can be debilitating, especially if it is a long-standing condition. Loneliness can be temporary – such as during a transitional life stage – or deep-seated, perhaps stemming from low self-esteem and feeling unworthy of others' company or simply having little in the way of friends or family. It can be sporadic: many adults – even those in relationships or with families of their own – suffer bouts of loneliness. It can come from living alone or from simply feeling misunderstood, even if you share a home with others. It can arise from having long-term pain or illness and not wanting to burden others with your ongoing suffering. It's often said that it's perfectly possible to feel lonely in a crowded room if you don't feel a connection with anyone around you.

There's a big difference between loneliness and being alone. Some people feel perfectly contented in their own company and feel stifled by crowds or even in the company of just a few people. Some find that time spent with colleagues during the working day is company enough, and that coming home to some time spent alone is a welcome break from having to connect with others. This is a happy state of being and is nothing to do with the isolation of true loneliness.

A good place to start if you suffer from loneliness is by finding opportunities to build up lots of short-term happiness, which can in turn lead to longer-term contentment. It could come from spending more time with people whose company you enjoy; cooking yourself your favourite food; having a really good laugh; allowing yourself more indulgences or working towards short-term goals. Is there a list of books you'd like to read? A show you'd love to see? A home craft project you're keen to start? An old friend you'd like to reconnect with? A cupboard you'd feel better for reorganizing? An exercise class you'd like to join? Try to build something you particularly enjoy into each day, even if it's only 15 minutes' meditation, a spell of internet browsing or watching a favourite TV programme. Some of these ideas are still lone pursuits, but they can take you out of yourself and put on hold the feeling that there's no pleasure to be had from your own company; other ideas encourage you to connect with other people, friends or strangers. And if the silence of being alone at home compounds the sense of isolation, try listening to a radio chat show or phone-in programme: it can be both uplifting and engaging to connect with people, even remotely. The same benefit can be gained from social networking, where you can choose who you connect with and find like-minded people.

Whatever the nature of your loneliness – and the causes can be complex and may even need unearthing through one of the talking therapies – concentrating on spending more time doing things you enjoy, even if they are essentially solitary pursuits, can help you to adjust to being alone, at least some of the time, and can give you a better appreciation of your own company.

Exercise 6

WHAT MAKES YOU HAPPY?

Use the chart provided on the next page to list everyday things that make you happy. Starting from today, mark a tick or a date in the next column each time you experience these things. Don't overlook even minor pleasures, such as getting an early night or catching up with a friend for a chat. The bigger things will come to mind readily. Completing this exercise regularly will give you the inspiration to repeat the same activities whenever you feel your mood needs lifting. The chart is deliberately longer than you can probably fill in straightaway, and is intended for prolonged use so you can add to it each time you experience a new happiness.

What makes me happy	Times I've experienced this

Summary

We've already covered a lot of ground and, having established your current level of happiness (or unhappiness), you have started to challenge old, ingrained thinking. You may have begun to look at your perception of happiness, both in yourself and in other people, in a new light. Although some of the exercises can be a bit uncomfortable – and all require a great degree of personal honesty – hopefully they've given you the enthusiasm to work on through the book. Keep focused on what you have taught yourself so far: that your childhood experiences don't have to dominate your adult life and that there is much you have already achieved that should make you feel proud; that the mind is an extremely powerful tool which you can train yourself to use more effectively; and that happiness can be built bit by bit starting right now.

Where to next?

Next up, we're going to take a close look at your relationship with yourself. You'll be challenging your long-held opinions about your personality and worth, finding forgiveness for your past mistakes and perceived failings and learning how to treat yourself more kindly.

My happiness journal

This space is for jotting down any thoughts, feelings or ideas you might have at this stage – it is purely optional.

→ **My thoughts on happiness at this moment**

_____

_____

_____

_____

_____

_____

_____

_____

_____

_____

_____

_____

_____

_____

_____

_____

_____

_____

_____

_____

→ My ideas for change

Your relationship with yourself

'It is of practical value to learn to like yourself. Since you must spend so much time with yourself you might as well get some satisfaction out of the relationship.'

Norman Vincent Peale,

minister and author of *The Power of Positive Thinking*

How much do you like yourself right now? If you answered 'Not much', can you remember back to a time when you did? Ask yourself what's changed. Perhaps a huge transition, such as becoming a parent, has made you a different person: for most mums and dads, for example, the carefree days of pre-parenthood give way to more practical considerations, anxiety about the future, a certain staidness in behaviour and changes to the dynamic of their relationship with each other. If you're not a parent, you may have undergone experiences in life that have effectively killed off the old you. This can give rise to low self-esteem, resentment and a sense of anger that was previously uncharacteristic. Does this sound like you?

If it does sound like you, try to remember who you were before and what defined you as a person. Who are you now? So-and-so's mum? Wife? Partner? How often are you referred to by your own name, especially when being introduced? Now think if there was a certain something that defined you before parenthood, whether it was your career, your fashion sense, your predilection for partying or your appetite for reading. Could you recapture some of your old self? Taking the time to analyse who you once were compared with who you are now should give you an idea of how much you've changed – and, if you feel less happy now than you did as your 'old self', then perhaps it's time to try to revisit that part of yourself and reintroduce some of the things that brought you contentment back then. And, by the way, do ask your friends and other half to introduce you by your name first, before explaining your role – and, if you and your partner are parents, don't call each other 'Mummy' and 'Daddy' except when you're referring to each other for your children's sake. It can lessen your sense of individuality and identity as well as potentially dampening the sensual side of your relationship.

Exercise 7

REDISCOVER YOURSELF

Look through your personal effects to rediscover the old you. School reports, work accreditations and appraisals, photos of old fashion styles and old friendship groups can all trigger memories of your former self. Focus on the positive aspects and see if you can translate them into your current lifestyle. How about organizing a school reunion or a gathering together of an old friendship group? Or visiting some shops or markets that reflect the sort of style you used to like? Maybe you could organize a trip back to some of the old haunts from your carefree days or deliberately make changes to your routine that will allow you to pursue a hobby you used to enjoy. Or how about downloading some of your old music favourites to take you back in time? Go back to your personal effects and use the chart to record how each item makes you feel, and then use the finished result to make positive changes. An example has been filled in to give you the idea.

Personal effect	How it makes me feel	How I can recapture this
Old school photo	Nostalgic, warm, appreciative of my friendship group	Organize a school reunion

→ Self-acceptance

'Accept everything about yourself – I mean everything. You are you and that is the beginning and the end – no apologies, no regrets.'

Henry Kissinger, German-born American political scientist
and former US Secretary of State

How accepting are you of yourself? Self-acceptance is a very hard discipline to learn, and yet it holds one of the main keys to personal happiness and contentment. How many times do you hear a little voice in your head telling you, in some way or another, that you're simply not good enough? 'I screwed up again' or 'Fail!' or 'No wonder people don't want to spend time with me' or 'How am I eating this when I promised myself I wouldn't?' Any of that sound familiar? There are so many ways in which we perceive ourselves to be falling short of our ideals. Now weigh these instances up against the number of times you congratulate yourself on a job well done. Chances are your inner voice comes down more often on the side of criticism than of praise.

Self-criticism – just as criticism of anyone or anything else – isn't a fact, it's an opinion. The same goes for praise. We may say 'This film is directed by X and is wonderfully entertaining', but the only factual part of the sentence is 'This film is directed by X'. The statement that it's wonderfully entertaining is merely a subjective opinion, and one with which others might well disagree. In his book *The Happiness Trap*, GP Russ Harris, who has a special interest in stress management, advocates changing the voices inside our heads to move the thoughts from opinions to facts. For example, instead of saying 'I screwed up again', you could change this to 'I'm having the thought that I screwed up again', and instead of 'How am I eating this when I promised myself I wouldn't', you could think 'I'm having the thought that I've let myself down'. These are, in themselves, statements of fact rather than judgements and, according to Russ Harris, they allow you 'to stay connected with what is happening, to be present, open and self-aware', without actually levelling a judgement. You enable yourself, in this way, to have a degree of objectivity you wouldn't otherwise enjoy.

Exercise 8

HOW SELF-CRITICAL ARE YOU?

Which of the following statements about yourself do you believe to be true?

→ I don't make enough effort with other people.

→ I could do better at my job.

→ I don't exercise as much as I should do.

→ I'm a talker, not a listener.

→ There's no point bothering about how I look because I'm not attractive enough for people to notice me anyway.

→ I'm always doing the wrong thing at the wrong time.

→ I should learn to cook better.

→ I don't make enough time for my kids.

→ I don't make enough time for my husband.

→ I don't make enough time for myself.

→ Other people are cleverer than I am.

→ I'm inclined to be lazy.

→ I could afford to lose weight.

→ I always make resolutions then break them.

→ My friends are so much better than I am.

However many statements you agreed with, practise changing your thinking so that they become, for instance, 'I'm having the thought that I could make more effort with people'; 'I'm having the feeling that I talk more than I listen'. Turning the criticisms into statements of fact – the fact that you are experiencing the thoughts rather than agreeing or disagreeing with them – puts some distance in between and makes them instead interesting comments that invite internal debate as to whether or not they're true. Allowing yourself to acknowledge and observe your feelings, however uncomfortable they may be, could be all that's needed to effect a change, whereas listening to a critical inner voice is not empowering and will help to perpetuate the same behaviour. (Remember the discussion about the long-lasting and damaging effect of childhood 'labels' from Chapter 1?) By analysing your feelings in this way, you may be able to discard them and move on with whatever else you were doing at the time they occurred.

→ Self-forgiveness

'To err is human; to forgive divine.'

Alexander Pope, English poet

Do you forgive yourself readily or set yourself impossibly high standards? Are you setting yourself up to fail or succeed? Of course, we all want to take pride in what we do and to be our very best – even if we don't feel that we're doing enough to achieve this. But although it's great to aim high, it's more important to do so by a series of achievable steps. You may think, for instance, that you're capable of becoming a bestselling novelist, even though you haven't any relevant qualifications or practice. There are very few people who have sat down one day and penned an overnight sensation, gaining instant fame and fortune. The most successful novelists have usually had some training in creative writing; attended seminars or courses on how to write; entered local competitions and submitted many a manuscript for publication only to face rejection. By the time they are successful, most have honed the art of sketching out characters and plots, researching their subject and setting themselves an achievable word count for each working day. So instead of starting up your PC with the express intent of writing the bestseller you just know you have within you, set yourself similar reasonable goals so that you can feel you are getting there step by step. Enter some short-story competitions, for instance, or keep a notebook with you to write down interesting observations that might make a good feature in a story. Otherwise, the likelihood is that you'll either never start or finish your book, or you'll face rejection after rejection by potential publishers. And how easily will you forgive yourself for failing in this way? You can apply this strategy to any career progression or personal goal.

Self-forgiveness is a natural progression from self-acceptance and equally hard to master. Most of us probably find it easier to forgive another individual than to forgive ourselves. That's because we crave their friendship – or possibly their approval – whereas we are stuck with ourselves whether we're generous to ourselves or not! But if you can readily forgive other people, why not yourself? There is so much more to you than your own, perhaps rather poor opinion of yourself. You will naturally condemn and disapprove of yourself if you're not achieving what you think you should be achieving, and yet you probably don't condemn other people for the same under-achievement, do you? Relax your ideas about yourself and refuse to believe the inner voice that criticizes you. Repeat the mantra 'I'm doing the best I can do for today' to yourself frequently. As long as it's true – and it may be that you're simply lacking motivation; have had a bad night's sleep; or just don't have the tools with which to work effectively, so feel that you're failing in some way – that is all you need ask of yourself.

Exercise 9

SETTING SHORT-TERM AND LONG-TERM GOALS TO BUILD A SENSE OF SUCCESS OVER TIME

What would you really like to achieve, in both the short and long term? Short-term goals could include losing a few pounds in weight; saving up for a particular coveted item; getting back in touch with an old friend; starting a book club; or spending a part of each day appreciating the world around you. Long-term goals might be to travel the world; to learn to play an instrument; to start an old-school association; or to run for local councillor. Whatever your own personal goals – and if you're not aware of anything specific, give it some consideration – write them all down in a special diary, with a projected deadline for achieving them. This can be moveable, as long as it's not because you're deliberately procrastinating: it can be hard to know exactly how long some of the achievements will take, that's all. And, of course, sometimes an unavoidable circumstance of life will get in the way: you can forgive yourself for these factors, which are beyond your control.

Use the chart to record your goals and mark off when you've achieved them.

Short-term goals	Date achieved

Long-term goals	Date achieved

→ How do others see you?

'When people say they do not care what others think of them, for the most part they deceive themselves.'

William Somerset Maugham, author

How do others see you? You have friends, right? So what is it they see in you that's attractive and pleasing? Try to see yourself as others do: examine the sorts of conversations you have with them and think what they might say. Are you a good listener? A brilliant empathizer? The one who makes everyone laugh? The philosopher people turn to when they're looking for answers? The best cook or host? The snappy dresser? If there are people who you know either dislike you or disapprove of you, ask yourself whether they are perhaps criticizing in you the things they actually disapprove of or dislike about themselves. This is often true. It's also sometimes the case that people look to others for the attributes they feel they lack, which is why some of the unlikeliest friendships can develop between people who are actually quite dissimilar. There will, of course, be some things about you that are less than appealing to others. That's OK – nobody's perfect. Acknowledging this allows you another chance for self-forgiveness, and an opportunity to think about how you might benefit yourself as well as others by making small changes to your behaviour. We all need to practise self-regulation in order to develop. This is a positive thing, not another stick with which to beat yourself up.

Exercise 10

ASK FOR FEEDBACK

Ask three of your closest friends to give you an honest written analysis of your personality, including any perceived flaws. Make it clear to them why you're looking for this and what you hope to gain from it. Let them know that it's important that you get negative feedback as well as positive (although they don't have to be too harsh in their presentation of the less positive aspects!) Getting this kind of feedback can have a great impact on how you regard yourself. You may be very surprised to learn about qualities you didn't know you had – and you can use the feedback also to work on any less positive areas. Don't try to become perfect, though: people love you for your flaws as well as your positive attributes. Believe what is said about you: not to do so would be to disrespect your friends. Write down somewhere private the three best things about yourself, according to your friends. Then write down three areas that are less positive and that you could realistically work towards changing. Refer to your notes often to keep yourself on track and to boost your morale and feel the love!

→ Do you like yourself?

'I don't like myself, I'm crazy about myself.'

Mae West, Hollywood actress

Most of us – Mae West apart – have mixed feelings about ourselves. Maybe you're over-analytical and have a tendency to rerun old conversations in your head to examine whether you may have caused offence; perhaps you beat yourself up too much for small failings; maybe others have led you to believe that they are doing better than they actually are and you feel you're letting yourself down. Now think about all the things you do that make you feel proud: perhaps you help out in your local community; maybe you're a generous tipper in restaurants; perhaps you're fantastically organized at home. Try to focus on these positives rather than dwelling on the negatives. They may seem like small fry compared with the achievements of others, but let's not forget that some people have a tendency towards exaggeration, especially if they feel in any way insecure. Any positive attribute – however insignificant it may seem to you – is to be celebrated. Any failing is to be forgiven. Think about how you feel about those people who accept you as you are: you could feel that way about yourself, too! The more you celebrate and take pride, albeit privately, in your positive attributes, the more you can grow to like yourself. Liking oneself is the key to building good relationships with others, and if you can be tolerant and kind to yourself, you'll find it comes more easily to behave in the same way towards other people. You'll feel happier in your own company, too, which is a really valuable attribute in itself.

Exercise 11

Go for a 20-minute walk focusing mentally on what you really like about yourself

Breathe deeply, walk tall, stride out and give yourself a positive appraisal. Aim to do this once a week if that's practical. Believe your own praise and focus on the warm feelings you can inspire in yourself. When you come back in, complete the chart.

My positive attributes

Physical	Mental	Emotional
my eyes	standing up for what I believe in	

Fill in the chart listing your positive attributes under each heading. They could, for example, include taking regular exercise; taking time out to meditate; being a supportive friend; and so on. Keep adding to the list as you gain new skills or think of more things. Whenever you're feeling as if you're not 'good enough', bring the list out and remind yourself of the many ways in which you are.

→ Your physical wellbeing

'The concept of total wellness recognizes that our every thought, word and behaviour affects our greater health and well-being. And we, in turn, are affected not only emotionally but also physically and spiritually.'

Greg Anderson,
US bestselling author and founder of the
American Wellness Project

How much care do you take of yourself physically? Do you eat a good, balanced and varied diet? Do you get enough sleep most nights? Do you take some form of regular exercise? Do you drink sensibly, having a few dry nights a week and avoiding binge sessions? Have you kicked bad habits such as smoking or other substance abuse? Do you have a healthy BMI (Body Mass Index: you can check this out online)? How often do you succumb to coughs, colds and other illnesses? Your answers will tell you what you need to do in order to take better care of yourself, and the degree to which you look after yourself can be a reflection of your self-esteem as well as your overall self-respect. When we are unhappy, it's common to indulge in pleasurable pursuits, but too often these bring long-term problems as well as the desired temporary relief. Consider how you care for your loved ones and what your reaction would be if you could see they weren't taking good care of themselves. In all probability, you'd worry, fret and try to persuade them that acting more responsibly would make them feel better. Isn't 'feeling better' what we're all trying to achieve? Yes, and there's an inextricable and proven link between physical and mental wellbeing.

There's another good reason to take better care of yourself, too. Kicking a bad habit, such as binge drinking, smoking or taking recreational drugs, not only removes an artificial 'crutch' that only serves to mask unhappiness rather than to solve it, it also makes us feel healthier and less worried about the inherent risks we're taking with our health. You'll feel much more positive about yourself when you conquer your vices and practise better healthcare, and your self-respect, self-esteem, energy levels and general sense of wellbeing will rise accordingly.

On another practical, everyday level, a few tweaks to your lifestyle can work wonders: a couple of changes to your diet here and there could make all the difference to how much good nutrition you're taking on board; bringing your bedtime forward by 20 minutes every few days for a week or so could gain you an extra hour's sleep a night eventually; finding a form of exercise you enjoy and can stick at takes more effort, but is worth it for the rewards you'll reap.

DIET AND EMOTIONAL WELLBEING

Did you know that what you eat can impact on your mood? Eating foods that contain essential fatty acids (EFAs), for instance, can help to lift your mood, so try to include some of these foods in your diet each day. Good sources include sunflower, flax and pumpkin seeds, fish, shellfish, hemp, soya and rapeseed oils, leafy veg and walnuts.

Other foods that are thought to have a beneficial effect on mood include red meat, dairy products, nuts, seeds, bananas, soybeans and other soy products, tuna, shellfish and turkey.

All are good sources of L-tryptophan, an important amino acid that facilitates the production of serotonin – a neuro-transmitter linked to elevated mood – and also promotes relaxation, restfulness and good sleep. One study carried out at the University of Vienna in 2007, looking at 42 industrialized nations, found that countries with lower estimated average L-tryptophan intakes had higher suicide rates. Omega-3 oils are also known to be good for mind health, and these are found in oily fish and seeds.

FITNESS AND HAPPINESS

Keeping in good shape is about more than just improving your body image or self-pride: taking regular exercise, for example, actually generates the production of endorphins ('feel-good' hormones) and can stimulate the production of serotonin for days afterwards. It takes discipline and determination actually to get up and get moving in the first place – especially in the winter months – but the sense of virtue you'll enjoy afterwards as well as the mood lift is so well worth making the effort for. There are plenty of studies that reflect the impact of physical exercise on mental wellbeing. Taking a holistic approach to our health – meaning that we take the body, mind, soul and spirit into account when we think about being at our peak of all-round fitness – is something that has been practised for centuries. As the Greek philosopher Socrates said in the 4th century BC: 'The part can never be well unless the whole is well'. We know ourselves that if we lapse into inactivity after a period of feeling fit and healthy, we can fall into a low mood, berating ourselves and feeling inadequate, guilty, unfit and de-motivated. This self-deprecation can lead to internalized stress, which in turn can produce physical symptoms, including stomach disorders, headaches and raised blood pressure. Conversely, making the effort to go and do some form of exercise, however small to start with, enhances the mood and not only has a physical impact, but an emotional one, too.

If you've fallen into the habit of taking exercise off your priority list, start by doing something today, even if it's only a 10-minute brisk walk. You don't need special clothes or equipment and you don't have to measure how far or fast you walk (that may come later if you decide to challenge yourself a bit more): just leave the house and go! Take your personal music player to help you set the pace and make the experience more enjoyable (but don't have it so loud that you can't hear traffic). Then, when you come back, congratulate yourself and give yourself a reward that won't undo all the good you've just achieved. Perhaps the promise of a lovely soak in the bath or 15 minutes with a good book will be all you need to keep you motivated to do the same tomorrow?

Exercise 12

KEEP A FOOD AND EXERCISE DIARY

Bearing all of the above in mind, try keeping a food diary for a month. Write down everything you eat and drink at each meal and include any snacks and drinks you have at other times, too. Ensure you include some of the suggested foods each day – and, if you're already doing so, try increasing the amount you eat of these foods. At the end of each week, record how happy (or otherwise) you've been feeling overall, how well you're sleeping and how relaxed you are generally. Maybe you could give each category a rating out of ten. See if you notice an improvement as the weeks go by.

Starting at the same time, set yourself a table of easy exercise goals, keeping the activities realistic in terms of time and your current fitness level. The top row has been filled in as an example. You can use the subsequent rows to customize and vary your activities week by week.

Monday	Tuesday	Wednesday	Thursday	Friday	Saturday	Sunday
Go for a 20-minute walk	Take a half-hour swim	Do 10 minutes' skipping in the garden	Go for a 15-minute run	Power walk for half an hour	Go for a half-hour bike ride	Dance to music for 20 minutes

As you start to feel the benefit of the endorphins and your fitness levels begin to increase, you can make the activities harder or more ambitious. Ever climbed a rock wall? Or how about taking a canoeing course or trying orienteering?

→ Do you give yourself enough respect?

'If you want to be respected by others the great thing is to respect yourself. Only by self-respect will you compel others to respect you.'

Fyodor Dostoyevsky, novelist

How much self-respect do you have? Ask yourself the following, giving real consideration to your answers. Circle the most appropriate responses.

▶ Do you live up to your own ideals? Yes/No/Sometimes
▶ Are you happy with your lifestyle? Yes/No/Sometimes
▶ Do you judge yourself fairly? Yes/No/Sometimes
▶ Do you ever put yourself first? Yes/No/Sometimes
▶ Are you able to say 'no' to people? Yes/No/Sometimes
▶ Are you forgiving of yourself? Yes/No/Sometimes
▶ Do you trust your own judgement? Yes/No/Sometimes
▶ Do you have your own opinions? Yes/No/Sometimes

All of these qualities are driven by your sense of self-esteem, and therefore affect how happy you feel. If you answered 'yes' to all or most of the questions, you're showing yourself a good deal of respect; if you answered 'no' to all or most, you have some work to do. You may have answered 'sometimes' to all or most of the questions, which shows that while you do respect yourself, you also have the ability to let yourself off the hook sometimes. If you know that you live by your own standards, you should also know that it's OK to allow yourself to let standards slide once in a while and give yourself time off from trying to win the approval of everyone around you. If you know, however, that you don't live by your own standards, perhaps you should ask yourself whether these standards are realistic – and whether perhaps you're judging others too harshly as well as yourself.

Your responses to the questions overall are a measure of your level of self-respect. If you are generally unhappy with your lifestyle or you allow other people to ride roughshod over you or make too many demands on your time, you're behaving in a manner you wouldn't respect in other people. And you wouldn't treat other people in that way either, would you? Consciously adjusting the amount of respect you show yourself will boost your self-esteem and you'll feel happier as a result. Part of this is about learning how to stand up for yourself through being more assertive.

→ Learning assertiveness, not aggression

'I am prejudiced in favour of him who, without impudence, can ask boldly. He has faith in humanity, and faith in himself.'

Johann Kaspar Lavater, Swiss poet and physiognomist

You may fear that raising your self-respect by putting yourself first more often or refusing to allow people to treat you like a doormat is going to require acts of aggression, but there is a big difference between being aggressive (which will win you no friends and is a very negative approach) and being assertive (which should earn you untold respect and is a particularly positive trait). You may know already – possibly by other people's reactions to you – whether you tend more towards aggression or assertiveness. Either way, it may be helpful to consider the following statements:

▶ 'If you continue taking me for granted like this I will make you pay.'
▶ 'I feel that I deserve more support than I've been getting and am going to put myself first a bit more.'

The first statement is a verbal attack on the other person, with a veiled ultimatum which would make anyone on the receiving end feel defensive. It's not only down to the confrontational language, it's because the criticism is aimed directly at the person ('you've been doing this to me'). This is the aggressive approach, and is to be avoided unless you want an out-and-out row on your hands, or are prepared to sacrifice the relationship.

The second statement is an expression of your own feelings, without accusation or aggression. By using the first person (as in 'this is how I feel and what I'm going to do about it') you're not apportioning blame, but are delivering a clear message of your own resolution for change. This is the assertive approach and should leave the other person feeling that you deserve no less than you've stated.

Try this type of assertiveness in everyday life so you get into practice for more important situations. In the supermarket, for example, don't mutter 'Get out of the way'. Instead, try 'I'm going to need to move around you if I may', again avoiding accusation and speaking in the first person. At a school meeting, avoid saying to your child's teacher 'What are you going to do to improve this maths score?' and try 'I think we need to work on this maths score. Is there anything I can do to help at home?' The problem has been clearly stated, but in a more sympathetic and cooperative way. (It's a clever strategy to get the other person thinking that the two or you are working together on a problem, even if you perceive the problem to lie entirely with them!) Wherever you can, approach any small confrontation in this way, giving yourself a few seconds to think about what you're going to say before actually coming out with it. Notice how the reactions you get are usually better than taking a more aggressive stance. Give yourself a pat on the back for behaving in a much more grown-up and effective way.

Another strategy people sometimes adopt in an effort to be assertive is to resort to sarcasm. So instead of saying 'No, I'd rather not go out right now,' they might say 'Do I look like someone who's ready to go out now?' It's a way of being defensive and is often used to make people laugh, but it can come across as an attack on the other person and is best avoided unless you're genuinely making a joke about a situation and know it'll be understood as such. It might be a hard habit to break at first, but if you find yourself coming back at someone with a sarcastic retort, check yourself, then say 'Sorry, that sounded really sarcastic. Force of habit!' and give a more straightforward reply. Think of the sorts of sarcastic comments you tend to make – or ones that others make that annoy you – and practise more direct, less 'clever' ways of communicating.

Exercise 13

PRACTISE BEING ASSERTIVE

In the chart on the next page, listed under 'Aggressive approach', are ten statements that could be seen as confrontational. Think of alternative, more passive but assertive ways of saying the same thing and write them alongside, under the 'Assertive approach' heading. There are no right answers, but you can use the examples from the previous section to give you ideas. Repeat these answers over to yourself until they feel more natural than using the more challenging language.

Aggressive approach	Assertive approach
I hate it when you behave like this!	
Can anyone actually hear me?	
It's not my turn to do the washing up. Get someone else to do it!	
I suppose you've forgotten that I asked you to lock the back door.	
Don't you dare call me that!	
I've had enough of being treated like a slave.	
Is there any chance you could possibly get up and do it yourself or is there something wrong with your legs?	
Oh, I BET you'd rather I didn't criticize you.	
What I say goes in this house.	
Left our keys at home again, have we?	

→ What makes other people happy?

'Happiness is not a state to arrive at, but a manner of travelling.'

Margaret Lee Runbeck, author

As discussed in Chapter 1, the things that influence our individual happiness are pretty diverse – and given that we sometimes measure our own contentment by how well others are doing, it's interesting to discover what's most important to other people. A survey carried out by the National Trust in 2010, for instance, found that 80% of Britain's happiest people have a strong connection with nature and the outdoors. The government's first happiness survey revealed that the top five things which make most of us happy are health; family and relationships; work; the environment; and education. Crucially, all of these factors are ongoing states of being, rather than the more fleeting moments of bliss such as sinking into a warm bath or enjoying a good glass of wine which, while they can undoubtedly make us happy in the moment, don't contribute to longer term contentment and the feeling that our lives are good enough. Perhaps more surprisingly, no mention was made in this top five of untold riches or even moderate wealth, although it's unclear whether or not financial status made up any of the questions.

Exercise 14

Hold a 'happiness summit' with your friends and discover the things that make them happiest. Note them all down – not just the ones that appeal to you the most. Just talking about being happy could raise your happiness levels and you may also find that you are inspired to pursue some of the things your friends enjoy. Talk and think laterally rather than sticking to the mainstream of holidays, drinks with mates, new shoes and job satisfaction. Ask them what their ultimate ambitions are; who they'd invite to their dream dinner party; what specific moments in their lives stand out as the happiest and why. Asking other people for their thoughts, feelings and ideas should spark some hidden desires within you, too. List them down separately and resolve to do all in your power to make them happen, either in part, if they're not completely realistic, or in their entirety.

Summary

We're ready to move on to Chapter 3 now, and you've hopefully taught yourself the importance of setting goals – both short-term and long-term – so that every achievement, no matter what the scale, is cause for celebration. Achievement makes us feel good about ourselves: one-offs are a good reason for a high-five; life changes are more likely to result in growing self-esteem and happiness.

Treating yourself with greater respect is another step towards greater inner peace, and that means looking after yourself better: mind, body and soul. It's too easy to put everyone else first, especially when you're fulfilling multiple roles, such as being a parent, child, sibling, partner, friend, employee and colleague! Stepping back and making sure you afford yourself the same level of care as you show others will not only raise your own happiness levels, it'll make other people respect you more as well.

Learning the (sometimes subtle) difference between being assertive and being aggressive is a great lesson for life and one to practise regularly. It can be surprising how often we fall back on sarcasm to make a point, for instance – and it can become quite a habit or even something we're well known for! But communicating with other people is so much more straightforward and effective when we speak out rationally and reasonably, and it's more likely to get a favourable result, too.

Now, are you ready to have a close look at your personal relationships past and present?

My happiness journal

This space is for jotting down any thoughts, feelings or ideas you might have at this stage – it is purely optional.

→ **My thoughts on happiness at this moment**

- watching my BBC shows

→ My ideas for change

Relationships past and present

'Love is that condition in which the happiness of another person is essential to your own.'

Robert A. Heinlein, author

For some of us, finding a life partner will be a one-off occurrence, but for many more there will be more than one 'significant other' in our lives. Each new relationships doesn't invalidate the rest, and it can be helpful to look back on how happy we were with our choices of each different partner; what made us happy in the relationship and what made us unhappy. There may be a repeating pattern that influences our choices, such as searching for a missing parent figure, pursuing an unrealistic ideal or seeking out abusive relationships because of low self-worth. On the other hand, we may repeatedly seek out people who put fun before responsibility, or who have attributes we lack but admire. Some relationships end through circumstances over which we have no influence, such as bereavement; others will have ended because of incompatibility or apathy. Sometimes one partner will fall out of love with the other and move on; this can create devastation for the partner who is left. Sometimes the legacy of a broken relationship is continuing sadness, and this can influence subsequent choices or even inhibit the pursuit of further relationships. All of these experiences build to influence our overall levels of happiness. At the heart of true love, nevertheless, is the mutual desire to make your partner happy. No relationship can be truly happy without this basic ethos at its core.

→ Have you been happy with your choices?

'Our soulmate is the one who makes life come to life.'

Richard Bach, US writer

Would you say you've made essentially good choices when it comes to finding a life partner? A well-balanced relationship will allow for freedom of expression by both parties and will be based on equality, mutual respect and trust. Take some time to really think about how many of your past relationships have fulfilled these criteria, and to what extent. You'll probably need to take some personal or joint responsibility for certain negative areas. Carl Jung, psychiatrist and founder of analytical psychology, said that in relationships we seek each other out subconsciously and then project our own fears and unresolved baggage onto each other, finally taking credit for our good side and blaming all the bad stuff on to our partners. Whether or not this theory rings true wholeheartedly for you, there's often a degree of this occurring within romantic relationships. It may have been a one- or two-way practice in some of your relationships and it will help to consider this when you're analysing them in the next exercise. There's no need for regret or self-judgement in this exercise (and there's a big difference between accepting some responsibility and beating yourself up); it's just helpful to carry out a brief analysis to look for repeating patterns or areas in which you've grown and moved on.

Exercise 15

ANALYSE THE HIGHS AND LOWS OF ALL THE IMPORTANT PARTNERS IN YOUR PAST

Work through chronologically, so that if you're in a relationship now, you keep this analysis for last. If you're not, ignore the questions concerning current relationships.

There is space in the chart for you to analyse five important relationships from your past, but if you have had more 'significant others' than this, copy the questions on to a separate sheet and continue your analyses.

Relationship 1: Name of partner:

What attracted you to this partner?

How important are these aspects to you now? (Very/somewhat/not at all)

How many of the things that made you happy do you have in your current relationship?

How many of the same negative aspects do you have in your current relationship?

What important and valuable lessons did you learn from it?

Overall happiness rating in this relationship (0–10)

Relationship 2: Name of partner:

What attracted you to this partner?

How important are these aspects to you now? (Very/somewhat/not at all)

How many of the things that made you happy do you have in your current relationship?

How many of the same negative aspects do you have in your current relationship?

What important and valuable lessons did you learn from it?

Overall happiness rating in this relationship (0–10)

Relationship 3: Name of partner:

What attracted you to this partner?

How important are these aspects to you now? (Very/somewhat/not at all)

How many of the things that made you happy do you have in your current relationship?

How many of the same negative aspects do you have in your current relationship?

What important and valuable lessons did you learn from it?

Overall happiness rating in this relationship (0–10)

Relationship 4: Name of partner:

What attracted you to this partner?

How important are these aspects to you now? (Very/somewhat/not at all)

How many of the things that made you happy do you have in your current relationship?

How many of the same negative aspects do you have in your current relationship?

What important and valuable lessons did you learn from it?

Overall happiness rating in this relationship (0–10)

Relationship 5: Name of partner:

What attracted you to this partner?

How important are these aspects to you now? (Very/somewhat/not at all)

How many of the things that made you happy do you have in your current relationship?

How many of the same negative aspects do you have in your current relationship?

What important and valuable lessons did you learn from it?

Overall happiness rating in this relationship (0–10)

Now read through your completed chart and make a conscious note to yourself to try to let go of unwanted repeating traits in your current or next relationship, and to try to reinstate the more positive traits in your existing or future relationships.

→ How's your current relationship?

'Our greatest joy and our greatest pain comes in our relationships with others.'

Stephen R. Covey, US life coach and author

How loved do you feel? So many of us continue in relationships that have either morphed from passionate to platonic or that don't make us feel truly loved. Some of us remain in relationships where we're made to feel worthless, unlovable or unworthy. In order to feel loved, appreciated and supported, we must feel accepted for exactly who we are. The same is true for your partner. Of course, the intense passion that characterizes new romance does eventually give way to a deeper sense of love, companionship and comfort: this is not the same as a relationship becoming complacent, dull or unfulfilling. If your relationship has dwindled, it doesn't mean it's necessarily time to leave: awareness of the fact, renewed effort on both parts, focusing more on each other or undergoing counselling may all put you back on track. The main question to ask yourself is: 'Is this a relationship that's mutually supportive'? To make things clearer for yourself, complete the following exercise.

Exercise 16

ATTRACTION THEN AND NOW

Make a list, using the chart on the next page, of the things that first attracted you to your partner, the things that endear them to you now and the things you'd like to change. How many attributes have disappeared or simply no longer appeal to you? Which list is longest? Focus on the current positives. Try to ignore or play down the negatives if they're petty things that don't have too much of an impact on your life. (Let's face it, no one's perfect and you probably have a few annoying habits yourself...). Start to think about how you could draw attention to anything about your partner that literally drives you mad or inspires dislike – making sure to use the assertiveness technique from earlier in the chapter. And remember: this isn't about you deserving sole status as the adored one; it's about finding a balance that makes you both feel happy and with which you can both live on an ongoing basis.

First attractions	Current endearing qualities	Maddening traits

→ Mutual kindness

'No act of kindness, no matter how small, is ever wasted.'

Aesop, Ancient Greek writer

This next advice applies to both you and your partner, so encourage them to read it too. How often do you say deliberately kind things to each other? It's so much easier to carp and criticize than to say something positive. That's because behind carping and criticism there's usually resentment, and by voicing this resentment you feel things are more likely to change than if you keep quiet. This is often not the case, though, as negative feedback has a tendency to spark negative behaviour anew. Praise is perceived by some as an unnecessary 'add on', but just because your partner is doing something well or making you feel good, it doesn't mean their efforts should go unacknowledged and unpraised. In fact, by praising your partner, you'll feel happier in yourself: you'll feel like a better person than when you're in nagging mode, and will be able to bask in the reflected pleasure you've just given freely. Another plus is that praise will often give you a much better result than criticism if you're clever enough to turn your complaint into something more positive. For example, instead of saying 'You always leave your dinner plate for me to clear away', try 'It's great when you remember to put your plate away without me asking because it feels more like we're sharing the chores'. This is a technique advocated by psychologists and it often gets results.

Exercise 17

PRACTISING PRAISE OVER CRITICISM

Psychologists also believe that in order for a relationship to be happy and fulfilling, praise and appreciation should outweigh criticism by around five times to one. How many of us manage to achieve this? Probably not many, but that doesn't mean changes can't be made, starting today. You don't have to be cloying or overly effusive with praise to make it worthwhile. Just try to inject a bit of 'emotional stroking' into each and every day. You could say things like:

▶ 'That shirt looks particularly nice on you' or
▶ 'It's really good you caught the earlier train home tonight' or
▶ 'Thanks for giving me the choice of what to watch on TV.'

Subtle, but powerful. Watch for reactions when you praise: hopefully you'll get some appreciation back and will have the enjoyment of knowing you've made someone else feel good about themselves. See how many pieces of praise you can give each day: at first it may seem contrived, but eventually it'll become a very good habit and one that brings you both pleasure. Chances are the habit will catch on with your partner, too, who may start to praise you more often, too.

→ Finding time for two

'There's a certain nostalgia and romance in a place you left.'

David Guterson, author

Remember when you used to anticipate seeing your partner with genuine excitement and how you wanted to spend every possible moment in their company? How you'd hang on their every word? Of course, this intensity of feeling passes – it has to, or no one would ever focus on anything else important – but it may be surprising to realize how far you've come from that all-encompassing place to where you both are now. How much one-to-one time do you and your partner make for each other, for instance? It's important to find some time every day to focus on each other: it makes you both feel appreciated and cared about. This, again, applies to you both. If either of you has a habit of inundating the other with a tirade of work-related anecdotes, moans or stresses, it's time to think how worthwhile this is. And wouldn't you rather leave work worries behind you once you're home, in any case? It's worth making it a house rule that unless something really radical has happened, such as a promotion or a firing, work talk must take second place to a brief personal catch-up. This could be a couple of statements or questions, such as 'It's lovely that you're home'; 'I'm looking forward to our evening'; 'How were the kids for you today?' or 'Let's have a hug'. Then, when you're both feeling connected and calm, try to find five minutes to sit and talk face-to-face about your respective days, making sure that neither one of you dominates the conversation. (If you have young children, distract them, if possible, even if it's with a short spell in front of the TV.) Each of you should practise reflecting whatever you're told by repeating back some of the messages within what your partner's just told you. Take turns talking, and don't interrupt. Just this small amount of time given to each other will make you both feel valued and important, as well as giving you a clearer insight into each other's daily routines, stresses and rewards. It's the lack of this sort of concern, attention and intimacy that can send one partner or the other in search of a more empathetic mate.

Exercise 18

REVISIT THE PAST

Pick a forthcoming weekend and plan a trip back to a favourite place from your early dating days. Organize it under your own steam or with your partner's involvement, but do give them enough notice to prepare: surprises are all very well, but in this instance it's better if you're both looking forward to recreating a little magic – and your partner may have ideas of their own to bring to the plan. If necessary, make some childcare arrangements so you don't feel under pressure, even if you only manage to escape for a few hours. It could be a drink or a meal at a favourite pub or restaurant; a weekend away in one of your home towns from childhood or a specific walk you used to enjoy. Spend time talking about your happy memories of the place together, and try to limit the time you spend focusing on other life stresses or the usual humdrum of every day. Much as it's hard not to talk about the children all the time, make a conscious effort not to go on about them: this time is all about the two of you. Remember when you were a new couple without a family? Go back there and enjoy reminiscing.

→ Rediscovering intimacy

'Sexual love is the most stupendous fact of the universe, and the most magical mystery our poor blind senses know.'

Amy Lowell, American poet

How's your sex life? It's so easy to let things slide when you've been together for a long time; this could be through complacency; lack of everyday intimacy; becoming more platonic friends than lovers; a change in dynamic since becoming parents or because you feel a lack of attraction, either to your partner or within yourself. Some couples maintain a regular sex life, but allow it to become predictable and routine. Others find they develop an imbalance in terms of libido, with one partner wanting sex more frequently than the other. An empirical study carried out by two US professors found that people who had regular sex with their partners rated themselves as happier than those who didn't. Because sexual issues are responsible for many unhappy or broken relationships, it's worth acknowledging any problems and making an effort to improve things. Even if you can't face discussing things with your partner, you could make up your mind to initiate sex more often or to find other ways of being intimate so that sex follows more naturally. You don't have to try and recapture the sex life of your early days together: many couples find a new pattern as their relationship grows.
If you can't face initiating sex, try making yourself more open to the possibility by suggesting an earlier bedtime or a mutual massage, or whatever you know may lead to intimacy. If your libido has taken a nosedive, try going along with sex even if you don't feel in the mood and seeing whether you do start to get into it: many couples have reported that even when they haven't felt remotely turned on to begin with, a few minutes into an encounter they've become aroused and happy to go with the flow.

Exercise 19

TAKE SMALL STEPS TO INTIMACY

To make physical contact come more naturally, start by taking your partner's hand or arm when you're out together, or initiate a morning and evening kiss if you've got out of the habit. Make a conscious effort to touch your partner more often than you do now, if only to lay a hand over theirs as they tell you about their day. Sit together on the sofa rather than taking separate seats; eat at a table, if possible, without the distraction of the TV or your mobile phones; go to bed at the same time, even if just for a cuddle before you go to sleep.

Sex therapists often recommend non-penetrative touching as a first step on the road back to good sex. You could start by massaging each other and cuddling, then progress next time to intimate touching, but without penetrative sex: this can be a very potent therapy as you'll probably both be longing to have sex as the exercise progresses, but you should agree beforehand to try to avoid this at first. (Having said that, if it happens, it happens – that's the longer-term aim after all!) When you've got used to being more intimate with each other again, progress to full sex, with each of you concentrating on the other person as much as on yourself.

If no part of the exercise seems feasible, yet you still love your partner, talk to your GP about a referral for sex therapy. You can attend these sessions alone or with your partner.

→ Practising team work

'Coming together is a beginning. Keeping together is progress. Working together is success.'

Henry Ford, American industrialist and
founder of the Ford Motor Company

Are you and your partner working as a team? It's common in long-term relationships for each partner to adopt certain chores as their own and to work independently of each other. This is fine as long as you are both happy with the balance and aren't becoming alienated from each other as a result. It may be that you could share the time spent on chores, and this can be particularly beneficial if you feel you don't see enough of each other or spend enough time together in general. Perhaps you could rethink who does what so that you can share some of the chores and come together as a team more. Could you cook together, for instance? How about getting involved in the kids' bathroom routine together? Is there room for some side-by-side gardening? Through sharing different responsibilities, you might even discover a new interest you can pursue further, such as joining a cookery course or visiting organized gardens.

Exercise 20

PLAN TO DO MORE THINGS TOGETHER

Lots of chores are more fun and easier to do with two of you working together, and it can help give both of you a better understanding of how much you each do around the house, too. Use the list to write down all the chores you do individually and as a couple, then see how many individual tasks could be transferred to the 'Chores we do together' column. Once you've got your list together, pin it up somewhere prominent and agree when you'll do what. Refer to your chart to make sure you're staying on course. (It's not written in stone and there will be deviations, but it's a good way of bringing things back on track.) A variation is sometimes to swap regular chores you do as individuals. This will give you each a better appreciation of what your other half does as well as ringing the changes.

Chores I do	Chores my partner does	Chores we do together

→ Accepting each other

'Truly loving another means letting go of all expectations. It means full acceptance, even celebration of another's personhood.'

Karen Casey, US author and speaker

Remember when you first fell in love with your partner? During that heady first few months, was there anything about them that had an effect on you other than enchantment? Chances are they had all the irritating habits you're aware of now, but that you accepted them or ignored them because love was all that mattered. The difference with long-term relationships is that the initial euphoria and love-blindness gives way eventually to a more level-headed affection – and the longer we stay with our partners, the more we take each other for granted, nit-pick at each other and try to make improvements. What's really hard to do is to let go of any built-up resentment we feel towards our partners and try to regain that 'warts and all' acceptance of them that we once had. It's worth trying, though, because one of the greatest ways we can show each other respect is by simply allowing each other to 'be'. Just being yourself – and being accepted for who and what you are – is another gateway to happiness. And by letting your partner just be, too, without constant criticism (but perhaps after giving small mention to things that really drive you mad, as discussed previously!), you'll find you feel more relaxed and happy in yourself than when you're stressing out and building up a head of steam for an argument.

There is a clear choice to be made here: we can either go through life grumbling and grouching at each other, or we can choose to ignore or underplay the less desirable aspects and give the majority of our attention to the good. When your partner irritates you for the hundredth time in a row, perhaps it's time to start ignoring that particular irritant: after all, if they haven't got the message after all this time, you're probably not going to change them. Instead, decide to focus on any little thing your partner does that's pleasing to you. Think about it, thank your partner, talk about the things you do that please each other. It may not come easily at first, but it's very worthwhile to try.

Exercise 21

PRACTISE POSITIVE AFFIRMATIONS

Therapists who advocate practising positive affirmations believe that we can actually think ourselves happier by repeating good messages over to ourselves on a regular basis. It can take a bit of practice to really focus on the messages so that they take hold of your subconscious, but it requires only a bit of time and concentration before affirmations become an ingrained part of your everyday life. Try giving yourself some positive affirmations about your partner to repeat to yourself every day. They could include 'I love [certain traits] in my partner'; 'I'm going to accept [certain behaviours] in my partner'; 'Our relationship is close and loving'; 'We make a really good team'; 'I first loved them because…'; 'What I love best about them today is…' or something equally affirming of your own devising. You could build this into a 10-minute meditation in the mornings if you have time, or take a few minutes out every now and then throughout the day to repeat the phrases to yourself. Before long, you should find that your attitude towards your partner is undergoing a bit of a shift in their favour!

Summary

Well done on completing the exercises in this chapter and having a brave look at your past relationships as well as your current situation. It's not always easy to admit to ourselves that we've made misjudgements or other mistakes along the way, especially when putting our trust and faith in another person is or has been involved. The aim of the progression of exercises was to identify any repeating patterns that may have occurred in choosing your partners, and to sift out the elements within each relationship that worked from those that had a negative impact. In doing so, and in looking at your current relationship, you'll have gained the insight to make whatever changes may be necessary for your greater happiness. To some extent, this will depend on your partner acknowledging the need for change and making a commitment themselves, but it's important that you take responsibility and initiate change yourself.

It may be that having completed the work in this chapter, you've come to the realization that your current relationship doesn't really have the potential to work for you, and that it's time to think about moving on from it. This will take time and courage, as well as a great deal of support from friends, family and, if necessary, a trained counsellor – but, ultimately, it should result in a happier you in the longer term, even though there may be a lot of emotional upheaval in the short term. Give yourself time and space as you plan to move forward – and do be honest with yourself and your partner when the time comes to talk.

Where to next?

In Chapter 4, we'll be looking at how much influence our own minds can have over our wellbeing. Often we are our own worst critics; sometimes we become aware that we're arguing with ourselves; frequently we set ourselves unattainably high standards or put too much pressure on ourselves. Only you have the power to change your inner voice – and this next chapter will give you the tools with which to start.

My happiness journal

This space is for jotting down any thoughts, feelings or ideas you might have at this stage – it is purely optional.

→ **My thoughts on happiness at this moment**

_____

_____

_____

_____

_____

_____

_____

_____

_____

_____

_____

_____

_____

_____

_____

_____

_____

_____

_____

_____

_____

→ My ideas for change

Changing your inner voice

'Be gentle first with yourself if you wish to be gentle with others.'

Lama Yeshe, Tibetan lama

The way we speak to ourselves can have a huge impact on how happy we are. Even if you've mastered raising your self-respect and repeating positive affirmations about yourself, you're probably still your own worst critic most of the time. Your inner voice will also decide how you view life's challenges – usually either as goals or struggles – and will also have an impact on how you see other people (perhaps not always as kindly as they might deserve). It can be useful to view your inner voice as an outsider, with whom you may variously agree or disagree: this can help you to be more objective about your thoughts.

We can try to change our inner voice by consciously stopping negative thoughts in their tracks and replacing them with more empowering or generous thoughts. It can be harder than it sounds because a lot of the time our inner voice is babbling on in the background of our consciousness, influencing how we feel and act, but keeping itself at some distance so that we're not always fully aware of it. In order to make a change we have to make time to stop and listen to our inner voice.

Exercise 22

STOP, LISTEN AND CHANGE

Choose a time when you're not rushing or hurrying. You could be doing a leisurely weekly shop; tidying the house or just sitting and relaxing. Now listen: we all have busy thought processes happening all day long, and your task is to tune in to what your inner voice is going on about. If you're shopping, it's likely to be saying things like 'Don't forget the milk' 'Do we really need crisps again this week?' 'Go on, treat yourself!' and 'Well, it *is* on offer...', all of which are perfectly reasonable. But listen more closely and you might hear, as a subtext: 'You care more about crisps than your health'; '*Another* treat? How many will that have been this week?'; 'Can we actually afford all this?' or 'Why do you never stick to your list'.

You might find the subtext thoughts reasonable, too, in this context, but there's room for more positivity if you just change the language. How does this sound instead? 'I'll buy the crisps, but I'm going to make sure I do some exercise this week', 'Not all treats have to be unhealthy or expensive' or 'I'm going to get into the habit of writing a list and sticking to it'. These are relatively minor changes, but instead of feeling like a loser before you even start, they put you in control of your own situation and – more importantly – show a good degree of self-respect. Don't be unrealistic in your new thinking, though. It's all very well to think, for instance 'I'll never deviate from a list again' or 'This is the last bag of crisps I'm ever going to buy', but these are probably unachievable targets which will only result in a return to self-critical, negative thinking if or when you fail. Keep to a script that's achievable and feel great about yourself as a result.

Some people find it helpful to visualize some sort of 'Stop' sign in their heads whenever a more negative or self-critical pattern of thinking starts to kick in. Others find repeating a more positive word – perhaps 'Reverse' as a reminder to practise reverse thinking – is a good trigger for changing emerging thoughts.

→ Practising objectivity

'The first rule is to keep an untroubled spirit. The second is to look things in the face and know them for what they are.'

Marcus Aurelius, Roman Emperor

Seeing the reality of a situation can be hard when we're personally involved or perhaps don't quite trust our own judgement, but it is possible to learn to practise objectivity to some extent. Say, for example, your inner voice decides that someone has behaved in an offensive way towards you (someone who, for the sake of argument, is a good friend whom you have always trusted and found supportive). Try to analyse the situation a bit before you necessarily agree with your inner voice. If you find yourself thinking, for instance, 'Her behaviour was disgusting', perhaps you could go over the scenario again, only this time with an objective and open mind, and come to a different or more measured conclusion. It can also help to try to see things from the other person's point of view; ask yourself why, for example, this friend who has always been a great support would suddenly turn on you for no reason. Perhaps by standing back and practising objectivity, the real truth of the situation will emerge, for better or worse. If you find it hard to see things from the other side – perhaps because you're too close to the situation or too badly hurt – talk it through with someone else whose judgement you trust. They may be able to give you some very useful insights that you would never have come up with of your own accord, or they may help you to organize your thoughts in a more rational and balanced way. They may, too, agree with you entirely. Depending on whom you chose to confide in, this could be a true reflection of the situation, or they could simply decide to appease you, even if deep down they think you're in the wrong: that's why it's important to choose someone who will give you an honest opinion. Once you've reassessed the situation, you may feel exactly the same way as you did at the outset, and with good reason – but even if you come off in a bad light, it's only when you can see the truth that you can respond appropriately, whether by having a reasonable discussion with the original friend or by climbing down and apologizing.

The way you approach life's goals and challenges can also benefit from a change of inner voice. Instead of saying to yourself, for example, 'Come on, lazybones, stop lying around and do something', make a conscious effort to change the message to 'Right then, let's get started. This is a challenge and you're up for it!'. This type of reverse thinking can apply to bigger goals, too. Say you've always wanted to go on a safari holiday, or to travel to Australia, but haven't been able to afford to do so. Instead of thinking 'I'll never be able to save up enough to do that', take out the finality of this rather pessimistic statement and say 'I'll put away whatever I can, slowly and surely. Perhaps it will be a present to myself for my [big birthday/retirement/other significant event in the future].' That way, you're not ruling out the possibility of a windfall, big pay rise or bonus, or change of life circumstances; plus it's wonderful to have a dream that may just be attainable. So by simply shifting the viewpoint from 'Why am I so hopeless?' to 'You can do this' you can create a highly motivational force within yourself.

Exercise 23

ON THE RECORD!

Use the chart to record your thoughts and write down a more positive way of thinking the same thing. For instance, if you think 'If I don't get this done, I'll never be able to...', write this down, then come up with something more encouraging: 'If I can just achieve this, I'll be able to enjoy...'. Or if you think 'Why am I being treated like this?', note it down and write alongside it 'There are always two sides to everything. Let's look at this objectively'.

My first thought was...	Change this to...

→ Make allowances for yourself

'Love is friendship that has caught fire… It settles for less than perfection and makes allowances for human weaknesses.'

Ann Landers, US agony aunt

The above quote applies just as much to our relationship with ourselves as to our friendships with other people: if we're happy to cut other people some slack when they fall short of the mark, then why not ourselves? No one does the right thing or reacts in an appropriate or accepted way all the time, and yet we don't tend to alienate other people if they let themselves down once in a while, do we? In fact, they make us feel better about ourselves when they do occasionally fail! Think for a moment about those people in your life who appear to 'have it all': they maintain a healthy weight, seem to make all the right lifestyle choices, are successful in their careers and appear to be happy with all aspects of their existence. How do they make you feel, really? Full of admiration? Or envious, resentful and a little bit sneery? None of these is positive, is it? And even if you answered 'full of admiration', the chances are this is mixed in with a bit of the less desirable feelings. Now think about friends who occasionally let themselves down. Maybe they give in, on occasion, to a bit of a fat-fest of pizza and beer; perhaps they've said something inappropriate at an office party; maybe they've rolled into work late a few times without a good excuse. How do you feel about them, really? Full of admiration? Envious, resentful and a little bit sneery? Chances are, none of the above. You're most likely to feel a sense of comradeship and a little bit of gratitude that they're not making you look bad for failing to achieve their levels of perfection. So why can't you cut yourself the same sort of slack by accepting that your very 'humanness' means you are bound to fail from time to time – and make other people feel more comfortable with you into the bargain.

Not feeling 'good enough' is a common phenomenon in this high-pressure age, but instead of beating yourself up, you could motivate yourself better by being a bit more forgiving of yourself. Once you've accepted that you don't need to win accolades for everything you think, say or do, and that it's perfectly OK to go off at the deep end, act a little 'out of character' or make a misjudgement once in a while, you'll feel happier within yourself and able to move on instead of over-analysing what happened – just as close friends and family do when they choose to forgive and forget.

Exercise 24

TREAT YOURSELF KINDLY

Next time you feel you've let yourself down and are stuck in a remorseful or even panicky state, instead of berating yourself give yourself a treat: go out for a coffee; buy yourself your favourite magazine; make a hairdressing appointment. Doing this is the equivalent of saying 'Come on now, don't feel bad. Let's make this better'. Taking time out to do something you enjoy will also remove you from feelings of guilt or self-recrimination and allow you some space to reflect on how you could do things differently next time. Punishing yourself won't make amends in any way. Conversely, although giving yourself some emotional 'stroking' won't make it all right to keep letting yourself down, it will help you to forgive yourself for your shortcomings, accept that they are a part of being human and pick yourself up again. Becoming more aware of our own human shortcomings also means we're likely to regard other people more sympathetically, which is never anything but a good thing. Of course, if by letting yourself down you have also created an undesirable situation for someone else, then you'll feel better if you acknowledge this and apologize graciously. (You really will!)

→ Learn from your mistakes

'The only mistake in life is the lesson not learned.'

Albert Einstein, physicist and philosopher of science

Yes, failure is an accepted thing, but it can only be positive if we learn something from it and move on. It's helpful to regard failure as an opportunity to learn and develop. There's no need to imagine that just because things have gone wrong for us in the past, we are bound to fail time and again. They key is to use past failures to help us aim for a different route the next time around. Consigning mistakes and failures to the past can be helpful, too. The only moment that is real for any of us at any one time is the one we're experiencing right now. All that's gone before has value in terms of shaping our behaviour, but nevertheless it's in the past – and the future is always uncertain. Getting this into perspective shows us that there's no real benefit in dwelling on past sadnesses and failures, unless in a constructive way such as through reverse thinking, which we explored in Chapter 1, or making a positive affirmation to counteract the disappointment, as described in Chapter 3. Accept, too, that it can take time to change, especially if our shortcomings are as a result of long ingrained behaviour. No one can significantly alter their inner voice overnight, and you'll have to remind yourself often before it comes more naturally. The following exercise will help to jog your memory as you begin to make a change.

Exercise 25

CHANGE 'CAN'T' TO 'CAN'

Next time you catch yourself dwelling on a negative aspect of your self-image, make a conscious change. So, for example, instead of thinking 'I'm a really bad driver', think 'I can take a refresher course and be a better driver'.

Then act on your positive thought and go and book that course! Get hold of a wall-hanging calendar and some stickers. Then, just as you would make your child a reward chart for good behaviour, give yourself a sticker each time you remember to change a 'can't' to a 'can'. You'll be able to chart your own progress and monitor how well you're making the shift in thinking. Don't dismiss the idea as silly or childish – tangible proof of progress is always worth having as a measure of success.

→ Embrace less-than-happy experiences

'That which does not kill us makes us stronger.'

Friedrich Nietzsche, philosopher and philologist

Accept that there are some less-than-happy situations that you can't alter for now – and that you'll also experience some sad times along with happier ones. It's all part of the human condition and, as described in Chapter 1, we all need to experience sadness or discontentment in order to really appreciate happier times when they come along. Perhaps you're the carer of an infirm relative; maybe you or a loved one have been diagnosed with a disease; perhaps your income doesn't cover much more than the mortgage. There are ways of improving many situations we think are unconquerable, though. Perhaps, for example, you could organize some respite care for yourself to get a break from looking after your relative; perhaps joining a relevant support group or online forum would ease the alienation that often goes either with being a carer or with serious illness; maybe you could renegotiate or extend the terms of your mortgage? Of course, none of these suggestions will resolve the situation you find yourself in – but sometimes there are ways, whether temporary or longer term, of alleviating the associated discomfort.

Whatever your particular circumstances, see if you can find some respite or support by thinking laterally and using the internet for inspiration.

All life's experiences make us who we are, and how we face and deal with the good and the bad in our lives also influences our overall happiness levels. Being in an unhappy situation doesn't necessarily mean we have to exist in a perpetual state of unhappiness. Even seemingly unalterable experiences often have hidden bonuses: having to care for other people, for instance, may be a demanding and unforgiving task, but the reward of knowing they are well looked after or that, in the case of an elderly relative, we're giving something back for years of care we've enjoyed ourselves, can instil a sense of pride and purpose. Carrying on in difficult circumstances, even when the going gets tough, shows us to be resilient and resourceful: both qualities that are worthy of celebration. Even if there doesn't appear to be any light at the end of your particular tunnel right now, your experience is very likely to be helpful to you or to others in a similar situation later on. Look for the hope and you're almost bound to find some.

Exercise 26

FINDING THE POSITIVE

By filling in the chart you'll make yourself think about what the positives are in your various tricky situations or circumstances. Have a good, long think and see if you can find the pluses, even if they're benefiting someone else rather than yourself: this is all part of the gift of giving, which is explored in detail in Chapter 10. The first row is filled as an example. See how many subsequent rows you can complete yourself.

Difficult situation	Positives (for me or others)
My elderly parent needs increasing and ongoing care.	I am being the best daughter/son I can be, and am bringing Mum/Dad companionship and comfort.

→ Don't be a victim

'The buck stops here.'

Harry S. Truman, 33rd president of the USA

It's so easy to put any bad experiences and unhappy situations down to something outside of our own control. How many times have you thought 'It's all so *unfair!*', as if everything that befalls you is somehow unrelated to anything you have brought upon yourself? OK, some of life's less fortunate events may come out of the blue, seemingly unconnected with your own actions – and this happens to us all – but other circumstances can be traced back to things we've done previously, ways in which we've behaved or choices we've made, in which case we must accept a degree of responsibility. But even when things are patently unjust, is there anything to be gained by assuming the role of victim? Whingeing on about the injustice of any situation, whether to yourself or a long-suffering significant other, is hardly constructive and will only serve to multiply and amplify bad feelings. (And what a lot of energy we can expend on complaining, huffing and puffing!)

Adopting the same attitude as Harry Truman, that 'the buck stops here' is one way of countering negative thoughts. Whether or not the situation in which we found ourselves is in any way fair or deserved, taking accountability for what happens next is empowering and will command the respect of those around us. Plus it galvanizes us into action, looking for the best, most practical solution, or at least some empathy and support. Once we've found that solution – whether it be temporary or permanent – we've gained some valuable breathing space for reflection, and should use some of that time in self-congratulation.

Don't dismiss others' attempts to help with 'You wouldn't understand': that is to assume that they have no similar experiences to draw on, which is often not the case. Sometimes the unlikeliest people have their own stories of triumph over adversity to share. Others may have had experiences that can make us feel things aren't perhaps quite so bad.

Exercise 27

EXAMINE YOUR WORRIES

Make a list of ongoing worries in the chart provided, and then try to think of some ways, however small, of easing the anxiety. Now write down and implement any of the answers you manage to discover for yourself, and chat your other worries through with a sympathetic friend – or note them down for further consideration at another time, when a solution might come to you more readily. (We can't always be in a frame of mind that's conducive to problem-solving and positive thinking.) Acceptance rather than resentment of things we can't change, as well as the knowledge that all unhappy situations do eventually resolve, can help put things into perspective and give us a more positive outlook.

Worry	Ways to ease the burden

→ Laughter really is the best medicine

'The most wasted of all days is one without laughter.'

E. E. Cummings, US poet, painter and playwright

There have been more scientific studies than can be mentioned individually which extol the benefits of yoga – and research has also shown that 'laughter yoga', which is a technique devised by Dr Madan Kataria, a doctor from India, combining yoga breathing with self-generated laughter, is extremely effective at increasing happiness levels as well as proving beneficial for general health and wellbeing. The technique works with the theory that even if you pretend to laugh or act happy, your body produces endorphins ('feel-good' hormones). This is because, even though we know we're forcing the laughter, our physiology can't distinguish between contrived and spontaneous reactions. The endorphins have lots of positive effects both physically and mentally: they increase the oxygen supply to the brain and the rest of the body; combat stress chemicals; boost the immune system; act against anxiety; help with quality of sleep, relax us and give us a 'glowing' appearance.

Laughter has been linked to pain relief, too. The American writer Norman Cousins, for example, when told that he was suffering from serious illness, credited laughter brought on by watching Marx Brothers films with helping him to manage the pain of severe arthritis. 'I made the joyous discovery that ten minutes of genuine belly laughter had an anaesthetic effect and would give me at least two hours of pain-free sleep,' he reported. 'When the pain-killing effect of the laughter wore off, we would switch on the motion picture projector again and, not infrequently, it would lead to another pain-free interval.' So break out your favourite funnies and laugh yourself to better health and happiness.

Exercise 28

LAUGH YOURSELF HAPPY

You can find classes and organizations concerned with laughter yoga by doing an online search. If that's not practical for you, try to bring more laughter into your life by meeting with friends who make you laugh; watching your favourite funny films and TV programmes; reading a humorous book or magazine; looking out a local comedy club or just recalling really funny events from the past. Social networking can be a great resource: some of the online communities where you can exchange ideas 'live' can be very funny, depending on who you connect with. The more opportunities you get for laughter, the more often your mood will lift and the longer you'll begin to sustain your upbeat mood.

Summary

This chapter and its exercises have demanded a degree of introspection, which isn't always easy, so well done you. Hopefully you'll have learned that even negative experiences have taught us valuable lessons, that proving ourselves to be fallible can make us easier company for others, who would otherwise feel unable to live up to our standards, and that, just as charity begins at home, we have a duty to treat ourselves kindly. In the mental exercises, you'll have taught yourself to turn some of your more critical thoughts about yourself on their head and to give yourself a break! Through laughter therapy you'll start to discover that it really is possible to think and act yourself happy, even when you're feeling low, and you'll have started to manage your anxieties and day-to-day worries by coming up with some practical plans to alleviate the stress. Above all, you'll have accepted that some stress, strain and worry is part and parcel of normal, everyday life and that it doesn't necessarily have to preclude the possibility of happiness.

So now that you hopefully know yourself a little better and are more on your own side, so to speak, it's time to brace yourself for a really honest look at your family relationships, how they impact on your happiness and what you can do to get the best out of them.

My happiness journal

This space is for jotting down any thoughts, feelings or ideas you might have at this stage – it is purely optional.

→ **My thoughts on happiness at this moment**

_____

_____

_____

_____

_____

_____

_____

_____

_____

_____

_____

_____

_____

_____

_____

_____

_____

_____

_____

_____

→ My ideas for change

_____

_____

_____

_____

_____

_____

_____

_____

_____

_____

_____

_____

_____

_____

_____

_____

_____

_____

_____

_____

_____

_____

_____

_____

_____

_____

_____

_____

_____

_____

_____

_____

Your relationship with your family

'Just because somebody doesn't love you the way you want them to doesn't mean they don't love you with everything they got.'

Thomas Jefferson, third president of the USA and author of the Declaration of Independence

Family relationships can be joyful, middle-of-the-road, downright tricky or, in some cases, non-existent, whether due to bereavement or estrangement, and some relatives are easier to get along with than others. But our experiences of early family life – or a lack thereof – as well as our present situation all play a part in the emotional shape we're in today. What's important is to embrace and nurture whatever family life you currently have, and this is especially true if you have children of your own.

→ Absent or dysfunctional early family life

'People who come from dysfunctional families are not destined for a dysfunctional life.'

Bo Bennett, US entrepreneur

If you've never had a conventional family life, it doesn't mean you don't have the wherewithal to create your own now. Perhaps you were raised in a children's home or have been repeatedly fostered, or maybe one or both of your parents were abusive, had a serious addiction or neglected you in some way, in which case you may find the quote at the beginning of the chapter by Thomas Jefferson particularly poignant: you might not have felt loved, but it doesn't necessarily mean that you weren't. Sometimes people, including some parents, are in such a dark place that they can only show the rest of the world contempt, although deep inside they feel love that they cannot – or dare not, for fear of rejection – articulate. You may never know the truth of the matter in your own case, but take comfort from the fact that the vast majority of parents experience a love for their children than runs far deeper than any words or actions can express, even if they are unable to communicate this.

If you're not a parent yourself, finding a partner with whom you want to share your life – or building up a secure network of good friends – can constitute having a family of sorts. If you have children of your own, it's a chance for you to break free from your past experiences so that you can create the kind of family life that was missing from your childhood. You may need some counselling or other therapy in order to help you to draw on your past experiences and consign them to an appropriate place in your memory, or you may already have broken the chains and started to live in the way you missed as a child.

We naturally look to our parents for approval and definition and acceptance, and if that's missing we have to define and accept ourselves independently – or, more commonly, look to others to accept us. Uncomfortable as it may seem, we need to realize that we don't, in fact, need the approval of others in order to feel confident within ourselves. As long as we're not deliberately seeking disapproval – and some people do, more out of a cry for attention than anything else – then we should be free to make our own choices, follow our own paths and feel at peace with who we are. The important thing is to acknowledge that yours hasn't been an experience you want your own children or anyone else connected with you to go through, and to build your own family life upon that conviction. Having a dysfunctional background is a prime example of where previous sadness or trauma can make way for happiness, and where you may find yourself savouring any happiness even more than others can because of the sense of perspective it brings.

Exercise 29

REORGANIZE YOUR MEMORIES

If you know a meditation technique, practise it daily. During each session, while your mind feels clear and calm, mentally consign your childhood memories to a special 'box' in your mind until you no longer feel the need to do so. You don't want to discard them forever, as it can be helpful to revisit them from time to time, both to remind yourself of how far you've come and to put other feelings or issues into perspective. You might find it helpful to create a document on your PC where you record the memories you want to put aside: simply typing them all out can be cathartic – and it also allows you to reopen the box physically and either review the contents or add to them in the future. If you find yourself unable to compartmentalize your memories and their associated feelings on your own – or even to recall them properly – you could perhaps explore the idea of having counselling or hypnotherapy to help you.

→ Happy early family life

'Happiness is having a large, loving, caring, close-knit family in another city.'

George Burns, comedian

If you're lucky, you'll have had a loving and secure childhood, and will continue to enjoy such a nurturing relationship with your family. Now you may feel, just like George Burns, that although you love each other dearly, staying in close touch isn't the be-all and end-all, and in some instances may even be more of a pain than simply enjoying the support from a distance. This can be a sign of great security within a family, and is something to be proud of. If this applies to you, the next exercise may or may not seem relevant – you decide. It may be, however, that spending more time with your family than you do currently would increase your sense of happiness. If so, aim to spend more quality time with them, both as individuals and as a group. It might seem hard to fit in any more visits or spare any more quality time, but there are usually ways of reorganizing the calendar if you remind yourself that your own happiness, as well as that of your family, will enjoy a boost as a result. After all, what's more important to you: having the carpets cleaned on a particular day, for instance, or putting it off for another week or so in order to accommodate a family get-together? As we've explored in previous chapters, happiness can be regenerated in your current life by including more contact with those who enriched your early life, so it can be a great support to reconnect with extended family members with whom you've lost touch over the years.

Exercise 30

INSTIGATE A GET-TOGETHER

Find a date, however far ahead, when the majority of your family (or, if you are without family, your friendship group) is free and make an arrangement to meet. There doesn't have to be a special reason or occasion – in fact, calling everyone together 'just because' is a good way of planting the idea in everyone's heads that you don't need an excuse to meet up. Make it easy on yourself by organizing a picnic in the park or a 'pot-luck' lunch to which everyone can contribute a dish. Suggest you take it in turns to organize a date like this at least twice a year – more often if everyone is equally willing. You could have a different theme each time, such as 'childhood photos' or 'funny stories' where everyone brings their favourites to recount and reminisce over.

→ Middle-of-the-road family relationships

'I know why families were created with all their imperfections. They humanize you.'

Anaïs Nin, French-Cuban author

Don't feel bad about not spending much time with less supportive or less enjoyable family members, especially those who are particularly difficult. You're allowed, as are they, to pick and choose how you utilize your free time – and the majority of it should be given over to pleasure if at all possible. If you value the company of 'trickier' family members, how about arranging one-to-one get-togethers?

Sometimes people can behave quite differently in a small, intimate setting than when they're in a larger group and you may be able to build a better relationship this way. It might be helpful, too, to arrange to meet on neutral ground. Going out for lunch or dinner, for example, can create welcome diversions as the other diners may inspire conversation and your waiting staff will undoubtedly chat with you, too. Also, you can control how long the outing lasts, which isn't so easy when you meet in your home or your family's.

On the other hand, if you have a long-standing weekly or fortnightly visiting arrangement that you'd rather not perpetuate, find a reason to break the pattern. Remember, you're no more responsible for other people's happiness than they are for yours. Maybe you could start a new class that clashes with the arrangement, or perhaps you could skip the odd visit so that it doesn't seem so 'set in stone'. You don't have to put an end to the visits altogether if this feels uncomfortable, just perhaps make them a little less frequent or regular – and, for all you know, your family may be quite happy to break the mould themselves. If they don't seem overly pleased with the suggestion, though, keep in mind that you are on a path towards greater personal happiness and fulfilment and that only you can make it happen. Ask yourself which alternative will bring you more long-term happiness: continuing with regular 'duty' visits or allowing yourself the odd day off from them, even if it causes offence?

Exercise 31

TIME MANAGEMENT

Fill in the two pie charts with each of the following categories: 'Time for me'; 'Time for chores'; 'Time for socializing'; 'Time for immediate family'; and 'Time for extended family'. In chart 1, apportion percentages of the chart to each heading, depending on how much time you currently dedicate to each. In chart 2, apportion the percentages as you would like them to be, then work towards making the shift. Refer to your charts from time to time to check you are still balancing things in this way.

Chart 1

Chart 2

→ **You and your siblings**

'It snowed last year too: I made a snowman and my brother knocked it down and I knocked my brother down and then we had tea.'

Dylan Thomas, author and poet

Most sibling relationships are built on a degree of competition, and include some rivalry. If you're lucky enough to have the sort of relationship described by Dylan Thomas above, where you have a bit of a roustabout – probably more emotionally than physically now in adulthood – and then move on as if nothing's happened, congratulations. This is probably the most mutually beneficial and supportive kind of sibling relationship, and one that's in all probability built on equality and fairness. Problems can creep in, though, when the competition turns into ongoing rivalry, brought about by not feeling equally appreciated, admired or loved. Having more or less successful siblings, for example, can make us feel competitive, which is another form of stress we can really do without. It's important to try to see yourself as an individual and not to compare yourselves just because you came from the same family. Material success isn't necessarily any better than fulfilment in other areas – and this works both ways, for you and for your siblings. The point is, though, that if you are pursuing a career and lifestyle that suits you – however 'elevated' or otherwise – that should be good enough.

Sibling relationships can be particularly significant and important for many reasons. They can provide a sense of companionship from shared history that is exclusive to you and them. Your early home life, whether happy or otherwise, is nevertheless a joint experience, and it can be helpful to examine certain aspects from an adult perspective: whatever your birth position, it can be eye-opening to see specific situations from the point of view of a younger or older sibling, and it may even alter your view of your parents and their motivation at the time. When it comes to caring for your parents in older age, it can be a great support to have siblings with whom to discuss various options, and to share the responsibility amongst you. Of course, it doesn't always work out that way if you are not all like-minded, and this very situation can give rise to bickering, disagreement and even family rifts. Your family set-up is unique to you, but if you value having a relationship with your siblings, there are steps you can take to make it the best it can be.

Exercise 32

CHANGE FOR THE BETTER

Answer the following questions to find out whether or not any changes you could make with regard to measuring up to your siblings would be positive or unnecessary.

→ Does my job fulfil me?   Yes/No

→ Do I have positive attributes my siblings lack?   Yes/No

→ Were any comparisons drawn by my parents
   justified?   Yes/No

→ Were any comparisons drawn by my parents
   unjustified?   Yes/No

→ Are my parenting skills as good as those of
   my sibling(s)?   Yes/No

→ Do I have enough money to live happily?   Yes/No

→ Is my home comfortable and welcoming
   regardless of size?   Yes/No

→ Do my relationships with friends fulfil me as
   much as or more than those with my siblings?   Yes/No

→ Am I happy with my achievements?   Yes/No

→ Do I have skills that make up for any lack
   of academic achievement?   Yes/No

→ Do I make at least as much effort as my
   siblings concerning my family?   Yes/No

Use your answers to analyse all the areas of
competitiveness you feel with your siblings. Spend
time reflecting on your own achievements and lifestyle
choices and decide whether you would be any happier
if you could match theirs. Try to use this analysis to
move forward, either to set yourself goals or to lay the
competitiveness to rest. You're all adults now, after all,
and have no need to seek the approval or parents or
siblings, or to measure your achievements against anyone
else's.

....

→ If you are an only child

Some children thrive on being singletons; others feel the
lack of siblings with whom to play, laugh and share worries
and secrets. Much will depend on your relationship with
your parents when you were growing up. If you were well
socialized with your peers and given plenty of opportunities
to make friendships you may have been perfectly content
to be the only child demanding your parents' attention
at other times; if, on the other hand, you found it hard to
make friends or you were deprived of peer company, you
might have felt a little bit isolated and lonely; and if you
spent a lot of time in the company of other adults, you may
have felt older than your years. All of these reactions are
common and normal, as is the anxiety that sometimes goes
along with being an only child. You may feel great pressure
to look after your parents; you might face difficult decisions
to do with their care that you long to share with someone
who has equal interest. It can be hard to feel that when your
parents are no longer around, you'll be the only surviving
member of your immediate family.

It can help to realize that being an only child isn't necessarily better or worse than having siblings – it's just different. Adults with siblings don't always have it easy, and family rows and rifts can be just as likely to occur amongst brothers and sisters as harmony and accord. When it comes to making decisions that affect the whole family, it can be hard to gain agreement from everyone concerned. If there's an estrangement between siblings, this can be as upsetting as feeling a lack of family around you: knowing someone is there, but doesn't want to have a relationship with you can be heartbreaking in itself. That's not to say that you should take comfort from other people's unhappiness or that all sibling relationships are fraught with tension – not at all – but just that the grass is not always greener on the other side of the fence.

Exercise 33

OWN YOUR POSITION

If you are an only child, you have a unique position with your family. Whereas adults with siblings may have struggled with being usurped as a previous only child, or being the eldest, middle child or 'baby' of the family, you have always been assured of your place and have not had to compete with anyone for it. There are many positives to being a singleton. Could some of the following be true of you? Reflect on these aspects from time to time, perhaps as part of a daily meditation:

➜ You may be more self-assured than your friends with siblings

➜ You're more likely to be resourceful and happy in your own company

→ You're less likely to be unhealthily competitive

→ You're probably pretty independent, not having had a sibling to follow or rely on

→ You are likely to be a strong, self-motivated sort of person

→ You could even be smarter than some of your peers, because your parents may have had more time to spend contributing to your education.

Celebrate all that is positive about having been raised as an only child and be proud of your individuality. There are online communities where you can talk to other adult onlies, too, such as Being An Only (www.beinganonly.com).

→ Your relationship with your children

'When I was a boy of fourteen, my father was so ignorant I could hardly stand to have the old man around. But when I got to be twenty-one, I was astonished by how much he'd learned in seven years.'

Mark Twain, author

There is so much scope for misunderstanding between parents and children – and it can be really frustrating when our own kids refuse to learn from the mistakes we made as children ourselves. Part of positive parenting, though, is allowing our children to learn from their own mistakes until they become mature enough to realize we genuinely have useful wisdom to share with them, as Mark Twain cleverly illustrates in the above quote. Until that point, some are more likely to do the reverse of what we advise, just because they regard us as 'sad', 'lame' or whatever the catch-word of the moment might be. But this is all part of the parenting experience and doesn't mean we're failing in any way, as long as we steer when we can and allow a long rein wherever possible, too.

We can bang on about having been young ourselves once, but our kids will probably never fully appreciate this, and every generation naturally assumes it's more streetwise, clued up and cool than the one before. However much we're motivated by unconditional love to guide our children, they are unlikely to appreciate the strength of the emotion or the sincerity of the intent until they become parents themselves. An important part of childhood is being allowed to go with the flow and follow the crowd to some extent. Our main responsibility as parents is to try and ensure that our kids are fully educated in the danger areas, such as drink, drugs and casual or unprotected sex, as well as offering a listening ear if and when they come to us for advice. However, there's a Chinese proverb that says 'Do not confine your children to your own learning, for they were born in another time' and it's well worth heeding, especially whenever we feel judgemental or condemnatory simply because we don't understand.

→ Mutual respect

'If you've never been hated by your child, you've never been a parent.'

Bette Davis, Hollywood actress

Are you happy with your children's development, attitudes and behaviour, and is yours a mutually respectful relationship? Respect has to be a two-way thing, right from the outset. Sometimes you can encourage more acceptable behaviour by redefining boundaries, setting up a rota of chores or talking to your children about how they could take on more age-appropriate responsibility. If you – or they – feel that you are too controlling, it can help to take your foot off the gas a little and allow them more personal freedom. As long as they repay you by adhering to any rules that go along with the freedom, you could all be happier with day-to-day life as a result. Having said all of that, it's also perfectly normal for children to rebel and you can expect rough times along with the smooth. Whilst this may make you feel unhappy, do try to regard it as a blip, and seek out other people who've experienced and come through the same stage so you can discuss coping strategies to see you through.

Rebellion is a perfectly normal phase of adolescence. Not all children are openly hostile or deliberately confrontational, but most will assert themselves or take an opposite standpoint from yours. It helps to think of it as assertiveness rather than rebellion, and as a healthy sign that your child isn't blindly accepting everything you've told them about life, but is starting to make sense of the world for themselves. Try to go with the flow: resist the urge to say 'I would never have spoken to my mother like that when I was your age'. It's irrelevant. Nit-picking and blatant huffiness won't alter their behaviour either; it's more likely to encourage it. It will all pass eventually. In the meantime, concentrate on the positive aspects of your teen's behaviour and your relationship with them. If they show thoughtfulness, even if it's only by making you a cup of tea or asking you about your day, you can rest assured there's love and affection for you there, even if it's not apparent most of the time.

It's not all about walking on eggshells around your teen, though. Living together means a certain amount of teamwork, no matter how hostile a proposal this might seem to them. Don't get into a row about it: make it clear it's not up for discussion. Everyone must pull their weight, regardless of their age or birth position – and that includes the adults, of course.

Exercise 34

ALL PULL TOGETHER

Get hold of an A3 size sheet of paper and a marker pen, then draw up a rota for family chores. Working together as a family, decide which chores could be taken on by which person, or organize a rolling rota so that the jobs change on a weekly basis. With young children, some small reward system can be helpful in keeping them on task. Praise them for their efforts, however small, and admire their work with pride. With older kids, you could offer some sort of incentive for taking on extra chores like washing the car or clearing the shed. The aim is to give each child a sense of responsibility and pride in their work. It's a tough call, but it can be done!

→ Talking with children

'If the person you are talking to doesn't appear to be listening, be patient. It may simply be that he has a small piece of fluff in his ear.'

Winnie the Pooh, creation of author A. A. Milne

It can be tough trying to talk to our children, as they often appear not to be listening – or to be listening superficially but not really hearing. Teenagers in particular frequently wear a 'Blah-blah-blah-not-this-again-I'm-soooo-bored' expression when their parents talk to them. But here's a thought: the key to overcoming any communication barrier is to listen more than we talk. Ask yourself how much time you spend really listening to your children. In the midst of trotting out plenty of our own advice, we can sometimes lose sight of the fact that they have worries and troubles of their own they might want to share, even if we can't solve them; and sometimes we can miss out on moments worthy of celebration just because we haven't connected properly or regularly enough. Don't forget, either, that kids sometimes come up with suggestions or solutions to problems we'd never have thought of, so it's often worth running things by them when you're trying to work something out (although, obviously, don't get them involved in anything particularly worrying or stressful). If your children are very reticent or find it embarrassing to talk to you about intimate stuff, is there a trusted adult within your circle of family or friends, or perhaps an older cousin or sibling they could confide in? How much happier our relationship with our children could be – and how much more we could potentially learn about them – if only we set aside a little time each day to communicate with them as individuals, whatever their age.

As explored in other chapters, listening effectively is a skill you can teach yourself. The art is to allow the other person to talk without interruption or any distractions, and without judgement, then to repeat back key messages from what you've just been told. Say, for example, your child describes in detail how he felt when he was left out of the football team. Keep eye contact with him while he explains, nod where appropriate, but avoid diving in with 'Oh, you poor thing!' or 'I'm going to have a word with your PE teacher'. When he's finished talking, repeat back some of what you've heard, to show you've understood it. So say, for instance, 'So you felt really disappointed when your name wasn't called, and you felt you deserved to be on the team. Yes, that's tough.' Only when you've finished listening should you ask your child how you can help. Say 'Is there anything you'd like me to do? Would it help if I spoke to your teacher?' then don't push the issue if he says no. End by saying you're always ready to listen to his problems. It's a powerful message and will hopefully keep lines of communication open, which will not only demonstrate to your child how to listen effectively himself, but in turn will lead to a happy and fulfilling relationship between you.

Exercise 35

MAGIC MEALTIMES

Agree on at least one day a week when you'll eat together as a family. Make it a rule that no techno gadgets can be brought to the table. Switch the answerphone on, turn off your mobiles and the TV, and chat. It might not come naturally at first, but after a time the kids will respect this family time and perhaps use it to seek advice or share concerns. If you can also schedule in 10–15 minutes to spend with each child exclusively every day, that will help you all to understand and appreciate each other better, too.

→ # Friendship with our children

'Stop worrying about being your child's best friend and instead worry about being their best parent.'

Bruce Sallan, US columnist, radio show host and producer

Whilst it's entirely possible to be great friends with our children, nevertheless it's important to keep some boundaries in place so that we are still in a position to parent effectively. Some parents describe their children as their best friends – and it's heart-warming to hear. There's a danger, though, of the lines becoming blurred: if we give too much leeway in terms of freedom, it can be hard to re-establish ourselves as decision makers and disciplinarians. Most children find boundaries reassuring, as they instil feelings of security, and prove that we are ultimately responsible for them.

The other reason it's important to keep from trying to be best mates with our children is that they need their own sense of individuality as much as we do. You may think that adopting their fashion sense, street language and opinions is a thundering endorsement of them as people, but it's not: kids want and need to be different from their parents – and you need to be different from them. They can only get in touch with their true identity through experimentation, peer influence and, finally, individuality and self-awareness, not by trying to be a 'mini you'.

The sort of true friendship that can grow between parent and child is founded on shared interests, family jokes, appreciating each other as individual people and making allowances (and this works on both sides!) It's not founded on raving to the same bands, sharing each other's clothes and knowing every little thing about each other. As our children grow into adults, this friendship may well keep on blossoming if we continue to resist the urge to meddle in their lives, and continue to support their way of living, even if it doesn't reflect our own.

Far from making you a happier person, trying to get closer to your children by emulating them will probably drive a wedge between you or make their behaviour more extreme in an effort to mark themselves out from you. For you, an increased sense of happiness is far more likely to come from patting yourself on the back for allowing your children to express themselves as individuals, and for giving them the confidence to do just that. As for you, it's much more fulfilling to be yourself than to struggle to keep up with all the latest trends, fashions, musical tastes and street slang, so relax, sit back and just be yourself. If you can be a great guide through life who is supportive of your children's need for freedom of expression, then you're doing a brilliant job.

Exercise 36

CHANGE THE RECORD

If you're guilty of trying to 'get down with the kids', then a subtle change in the way you communicate with them could make a difference to their sense of freedom and individuality. Here's a chart of some of the things you may have found yourself saying to your kids, and things you could say instead.

Instead of saying...	Try this...
I love this band! Lend me your CD.	I love that you've found your own taste in music.
Can I wear your leggings tonight?	You have a good sense of style.
Can I be Facebook friends with your mates?	I'm glad you have a great circle of friends
Why are you shutting your bedroom door? It's only me!	You're right to want a bit of privacy – everyone does.
Do you think I'm cool?	I like that we're all happy being ourselves.

OK, so these probably aren't all typical statements you've made, but you get the idea. Back off: most kids whose parents are trying to be cool are absolutely mortified. If you do recognize yourself in this sort of behaviour, revisit *Your relationship with yourself* in Chapter 2 and try the exercise *Rediscover yourself* again to boost your own self-confidence. This is going to make you a whole lot happier than embarrassing your kids – and, in doing so, yourself.

Summary

The aim of this chapter was to get you to look at the dynamics within your family from several different aspects: firstly, from the perspective of your childhood and how your relationships evolved; then from your adult viewpoint, and how this growing up may (or may not) have affected the way you view your parents, your siblings or yourself as an only child; then your relationship with your own children and how much your early influences have affected your own parenting style. It should have proven to be something of an eye-opener, and allowed you to stand outside of yourself for a bit and regard your family history and set-up as more of an outsider. From this standpoint it's easier to see that the way we react and respond to family now doesn't necessarily need to be the same as it was in childhood or adolescence, and that it may be more appropriate – and easier – to approach things in a different way. You'll have taught yourself how to make the best of your different inter-family relationships and how to field and handle more difficult relatives to everyone's advantage.

Where to next?

Now it's time to examine your relationships with your friends; who you choose to surround yourself with and why; how fulfilling your friendships are for you; and what opportunities may be open to you for forging new friendships.

My happiness journal

This space is for jotting down any thoughts, feelings or ideas you might have at this stage – it is purely optional.

→ **My thoughts on happiness at this moment**

_____

_____

_____

_____

_____

_____

_____

_____

_____

_____

_____

_____

_____

_____

_____

_____

_____

_____

→ My ideas for change

_____

_____

_____

_____

_____

_____

_____

_____

_____

_____

_____

_____

_____

_____

_____

_____

_____

_____

_____

_____

_____

_____

_____

_____

_____

_____

_____

_____

_____

_____

_____

_____

_____

Friendship choices and your happiness

'True happiness consists not in the multitude of friends, but in their worth and choice.'

Samuel Johnston, British lexicographer

For many of us, friends play at least as important a role in our lives as family, and our choice of friends can speak volumes about our own self-esteem and happiness. The best friendships are mutually supportive, non-judgemental and enduring of hardship, and are an illustration of your equality and self-esteem; less fulfilling friendships, on the other hand, which are imbalanced in favour of the other person, can reflect your low self-worth. In other cases, friendships can be all about dependency – and if you have friends you feel lean on you too much, it's worth examining your reasons for perpetuating these relationships. But part of fulfilling your own happiness is not to 'cut out the dead wood' if you feel that there is value to your friendships, even if they seem a bit one-way with you offering more support than you receive (and for some people this is reward enough, which will be explored in a later chapter); no, it's to find a way to break with or distance yourself from friends and acquaintances who judge you, try to control you, give little, bring you down or give you reason to doubt yourself in any way – or to address the issues by explaining why you're not finding the relationship fulfilling. It's not easy to break ties with people who've been in your life long term, but it can be done without making them feel that you are abandoning or rejecting them out of hand. Think about how you might be able to spend more time with more affirming people or on more rewarding occupations so that there's simply less time to devote to unfulfilling relationships – and how to keep some time, if it makes you feel good, for those people who are most deserving and appreciative of your support. Let's look at how you can try to build your support network by re-establishing contact with people who've meant a lot to you in the past.

→ Your friendships from school and college

'There was never any substitute for those friendships of childhood that survive into adult years. Those are the ones in which we are bound to one another with hoops of steel.'

Alexander McCall Smith, author

If you're lucky enough to keep contact with and enjoy the company of friends you first met in school or elsewhere in your childhood, you're fortunate indeed. All that shared history is something for which there's no substitute – although it's fair to say that some things may be best left buried in the past! If your friends are good friends, though, they'll understand that and know which territory to leave alone. Keeping in touch with our oldest friends can feel like an extension of our own families, especially if we've got to know their extended families over the years, too. Sometimes an old friend's parents can be a very valuable source of comfort and advice if we have either lost our own or aren't as close as we might be.

If you haven't kept contact with friends from childhood, they might still be glad to hear from you now – and getting back in touch could evoke all sorts of happy memories, if those were happy times for you. Even if you were unhappy as a child, your old mates might be able to put things into perspective for you now that you're all adults. Perhaps you were bullied in school and have always secretly thought yourself unworthy because of the experience? Maybe now is the time to get in touch with a couple of people who were there at the time, and to gain their adult perspective on what went wrong. You won't necessarily get answers, especially as it might be hard to look at the situation with new eyes after all this time, but just the feeling of being accepted by your old friends, and the knowledge that you're all grown-ups who moved on long ago, might help you to bury this particular bad memory once and for all. You may even be brave enough to contact the perpetrator, perhaps through a social network, and talk to them about what motivated them to bully you: it's a big ask, but you may well discover that your bully was in a far less happy situation than you were, and that there was some underlying reason for their behaviour that you'll be able to excuse as an adult. These meetings can be very cathartic and contribute to a sense of new acceptance and wellbeing.

Sometimes our dearest friends are people we weren't drawn to right away. If you went to college or university, some of the friends you made there may have turned out to be friends for life – and yet they may not have been the people you connected with immediately, or even those you spent most of your time with. Sometimes the friends we thought would stand by us through thick and thin flee at the first sign we need their support; and sometimes true friendship comes from people we'd never have expected. Because so much shaping of our characters, our changing politics, sexual awakening and self-discovery happens during these highly formative years, it can feel as if our true friends know us as well as – or better than – our own families. The fledgling years of further education should have enabled us, over the years, to spend time reflecting on our own personalities, our strengths and weaknesses, our general take on life and who we would like to be as adults, and the true friendships forged during this time can contribute greatly to our ongoing happiness.

If your experience of college or university was not happy and you felt either marginalized, ignored or isolated, you may prefer to put the memory of these years behind you. But just before you do, think whether there was one single person – a co-student, lecturer or tutor – whose company you found fulfilling and enjoyable. Could you benefit from getting back in touch, even if only for a one-off catch-up?

Exercise 37

SEEK OUT LONG-LOST FRIENDS

There are so many social networking websites through which it's possible to trace people that you should be able to find at least some of your old friends from an earlier phase of your life. If you can't find contact details for the specific people you're trying to track down, you could try approaching other friends of theirs to see if they can put you in touch. It might be best to set up a separate networking page from your own personal profile, though, and give it a group name, just in case you attract unwanted attention or find that your rediscovered mates are a bit too keen! Use the list below to start noting down people you'd really like to see again. Try to remember well back into the past and think about your happiest memories and who they involved.

Name of contact	Contact made? ✓ or ✗

→ Family friends

'I believe that we are always attracted to what we need most, an instinct leading us towards the persons who are to open new vistas in our lives and fill them with new knowledge.'

Helene Iswolsky, translator

How many of your parents' friends are you still in touch with? Sometimes family friends can be an extension of the family: in the same way that your oldest friends from childhood have a huge shared history with you, so do they – only their memories of you may be more extensive or even totally different from those of your friends. Perhaps they had a keener interest in your after-school hobbies or your academic progress; perhaps they were amongst the first people to teach you new skills and games or to really listen to your point of view. Perhaps they can fill in memories for you where you have blanks, or throw light on any family problems you may have had but were too young to understand at the time. Maybe you were able to communicate with them in ways that wouldn't have been so comfortable with your parents; or perhaps they took you on days out or even holidays with their own children that added to your cherished childhood memories.

Just because we're adults doesn't mean there is no longer any value to our family friends. OK, it may feel as if staying in touch with them – especially if our own parents are no longer around – is something of a burdensome duty, but have you considered that they might be another source of valuable friendship in adulthood, too, or that they could contribute new knowledge about our parents or our early lives in childhood? If you haven't had much contact with them in adulthood, you might even find that you can build a whole new kind of fulfilling relationship, based on adult values and shared views. What of their kids? Are their lives so different from your own that it's really not worth getting in touch? You might find that by re-establishing contact with your parents' friends you reconnect with their children who, still a similar age to you, can offer valuable friendship. Can you see a pattern emerging of the role of historic friendships in long-term happiness?

Exercise 38

GET BACK IN TOUCH!

Ask your parents if they'd mind if you got back in touch with their friends: perhaps offer to organize a coffee morning or afternoon tea gathering so you can all get together. It's probably easiest if your parents are there at least the first time round. You might find their presence is most welcome at all your meetings: to be socializing with your parents and their friends could introduce another dimension of friendship and make you feel more valuable to your parents as a fully-fledged adult, rather than being regarded as their 'grown-up child', which is rather different. If your parents are no longer around, see if you can find contact numbers for their friends, then make some tentative phone calls to see if it feels right to get together. You don't have to set a regular arrangement in stone now or at any time in the future unless you want to.

→ Workplace friends

'Individually we are one drop. Together we are an ocean.'

Ryunosuke Satoro, Japanese poet

Most of us will change career or at least job several times in our lives: according to one UK-based careers advice agency, statistics show that on average a person will have between 10–14 different jobs over their lifetime, involving three to four career changes. Workmates can become great friends, even when we no longer work with them – in fact, it's often even better when we no longer work with them, as there's no reason for rivalry or mistrust. The aspect of shared interest, along with the camaraderie that goes with working together can bring people close and offer mutual support as well as companionship outside of working hours. But even if we don't choose to socialize with workmates outside of the workplace, their friendship is nevertheless valuable. In some ways, it can be great to have friends who only know you as a colleague and who don't share the rest of your life: you can keep a part of yourself separate and even be a slightly different person at work if you want to. Maybe you feel more 'grown up' at work and less defined as someone's mum or partner; or perhaps your life at work feels like an escape from any worries you have at home and you prefer to keep it that way. There's something to be said for keeping a little 'professional distance', as work-home crossover can affect the way your workmates view you and may even cost you a promotion or your job if you fall out with someone who was previously your friend and in whom you've confided.

The point about workplace friendships is that increasing your personal happiness means getting the most out of all opportunities for pleasure, and that includes every type of friendship group, as well as your own personal fulfilment at work.

Exercise 39

DO SOME LOW-KEY NETWORKING

Make a point of having a social conversation with a new person in your workplace each day this week. It doesn't have to result in having lunch together or going for a beer after work; it just has to be non work-related. So an opener might be 'Did you see that programme on TV last night?' or 'What a great weekend I just had. How was yours?' Even if it doesn't come naturally at first, you'll soon raise your profile as a more gregarious and friendlier person. Each time you succeed in engaging a new contact in conversation, give yourself a small treat or at least a big mental pat on the back. In time this could progress to instigating some lunchtime or after-work meet-ups: maybe a weekly coffee, a lunchtime run or some group trips to the gym.

→ Friends of friends

'I awoke this morning with devout thanksgiving for my friends, the old and the new.'

Ralph Waldo Emerson, American essayist and poet

Some people can be incredibly possessive of their own friends and are not happy to share them with others; some people are happy to share, but only as long as they can be part of all future meet-ups; other people are happy to introduce some friends to others and watch new friendships flourish between those they've brought together, regardless of whether they're always included in future arrangements. The second or third scenarios are both of value: after all, if you particularly enjoy the company of a friend-of-a-friend, but the implication is that you only meet all together, you're still getting more enjoyment than by not having that connection at all. The third scenario, though, where generous friends are happy for you to strike up your own separate friendships with their mates, can create a wonderful opportunity for broadening your social network. Don't write off the possibility: when someone you know and respect likes someone else, that's got to be a pretty good endorsement.

Exercise 40

IT'S WHO YOU KNOW...

You may have to be proactive, as it might not occur to your mates to bring you into their wider groups, so what about getting the ball rolling yourself? Invite one of your more generous mates whose friends you know and admire to meet up with one of two of your own friends you know they'll get along with. If all goes well, see if there's anyone in their network they think you'd get along with, ask for an introduction and take it from there. You might even find you build other crossover groups with loads more potential for socializing and closeness.

→ ## Neighbours as friends

'Love thy neighbour – but don't pull down your hedge.'

Benjamin Franklin, American statesman, scientist and philosopher

Some of the most enduring friendships are formed between neighbours, but it's advisable to be cautious about becoming over-friendly, especially with next door. Future problems over party walls, other shared property, building works and noise can be really tricky to bring up and resolve if you've previously been great friends. This doesn't mean you should rule out the possibility – just that you might have to be prepared to get your fingers burnt at a later date if one or other of you suddenly steps over the somewhat hazy line where neighbourliness and friendship cross over.

Certainly it's great to make friends within your neighbourhood: it means there's often a listening ear or a social opportunity literally just around the corner, and there's nothing like actually spending time with a friend face-to-face without having to make big plans or travel a distance to get there. Local friends know and understand local concerns, too, and are likely to band together to lobby their MP or start up a petition if they all object to any local controversy. They might also agree to setting up a babysitting circle, joining a gym class together or just having regular 'socials'. There'll always be some local burning issue to talk about with neighbourhood friends – and who's to say these relationships won't grow into something more?

Another beauty of neighbourly friendships is that they can involve more-or-less equal amounts of give and take. And even if the situation is a little weighted towards you doing more giving than taking, it can be very rewarding and spawn its own happiness to do good deeds without expecting a reward – more of which in Chapter 10.

→ The wider community and friendship possibilities

'How does one keep from "growing old inside"? Surely only in community. The only way to make friends with time is to stay friends with people.'

Robert McAfee Brown, US theologian

If you don't particularly gel with any of your near neighbours and feel a little shy, how about trying to join some local groups that might interest you? You can look them up on online directories and chat forums, ask at your local library or look at the notices in shop windows and on supermarket noticeboards. There might a debating group, an art-lovers' group, a walking or cycling group or any number of other groups of interest. If not, are you brave enough (and could it mark the beginning of a new you?) to start one up yourself? Put an online notice on some local chat forums or advertise on a noticeboard yourself, proposing the idea of getting a group of like-minded people together on neutral ground. (Don't invite strangers to your home first off: you might find yourself lumbered with people who don't inspire you, or – worse still – who are really bothersome.) Leave your mobile phone number and wait for a response. Or, depending on your gender, taste, age and interests, how about finding out about the local Women's Institute (WI)? They're not all about home-made jam and scones – far from it. In fact, they can be quite influential and often have interesting guest speakers, organize days out, have different topics for discussion at each meeting and generally get involved with and contribute to the wider community. Some groups offer 'taster' sessions for a minimal charge before you sign up to join – and even if you go along and meet only one other person you'd like to stay in touch with, you'll have started a potential new friendship.

Exercise 41

MAKE USE OF ONLINE RESOURCES

As well as using the internet as a way of searching for specific people, another way of networking that's grown in popularity enormously is 'tweeting'. By signing up to www.twitter.com, you can post live online soundbites, and you can find like-minded people from all sorts of backgrounds and regions to exchange ideas with. It can feel as if you're in good company when you interact in real time, especially when regular users build a relationship with you. Some people start their own 'hashtag' games for everyone to join in with; others publish links to news stories and topical events; some just post about what they're doing at the time (although you'll get a better response if the posts are more interesting than just 'Eating my dinner', for instance). If you think tweeting is the way forward for you, try to be as interesting and engaging as you can for maximum interaction and ongoing contact. You don't have to use your real name if you'd rather not be identified. There are other similar websites offering a similar service, so go on, find one you like and sign up. One word of caution: the most recent results of an annual divorce survey published by UK chartered accountants Grant Thornton warns that overuse of social networking is heavily cited as a reason for divorce, so get the balance right and take care not to let it take over all your social time!

Summary

It can be very revealing and quite challenging to examine friendships in such detail – but it can also be affirming and reassuring. During this chapter you'll have discovered the different levels of significance various friendships have for you; that sometimes specific friends are valuable in specific ways; that there is no obligation for you to continue friendships that are no longer fulfilling for you; that there are perhaps more opportunities for you to make new friendships than had previously occurred to you and that friendships can be as important if not more so than family relationships.

Where to next?

The next chapter looks at your relationship with material things and money, and that part they play in your overall happiness. You might find you have changed your views on materialism and possessions one way or another by the end of the chapter and its exercises. There's only one way to find out: onwards!

My happiness journal

This space is for jotting down any thoughts, feelings or ideas you might have at this stage – it is purely optional.

→ **My thoughts on happiness at this moment**

_____

_____

_____

_____

_____

_____

_____

_____

_____

_____

_____

_____

_____

_____

_____

_____

_____

_____

_____

_____

→ My ideas for change

_____

_____

_____

_____

_____

_____

_____

_____

_____

_____

_____

_____

_____

_____

_____

_____

_____

_____

_____

_____

_____

_____

_____

_____

_____

_____

_____

_____

_____

Materialism and happiness

'Happiness comes from spiritual wealth, not material wealth... Happiness comes from giving, not getting.'

John Templeton, US investor and philanthropist

Can money buy you happiness? We're frequently told that it can't, but according to a recent report, *The Pursuit of Happiness* by the Institute of Economic Affairs, money – and plenty of it – does, in fact, make us happier than anything else. Without a doubt it can help to facilitate things that will make us happy. Wealth in itself, though, doesn't always bring contentment, and in some cases excessive wealth can be ultimately destructive – especially if it comes suddenly and without the effort of earning it. You only have to sweep the internet and you'll find stories of lottery winners whose big wins have led to despair, either through sudden publicity and thousands of begging letters; through being unable to cope with the sheer responsibility of having so much money, or by adopting a 'spend, spend, spend' mentality that can lead, in the end, to destitution. Others can find fulfilment from new-found wealth, especially if it enables them to pursue a lifelong dream or to help others. Money can certainly enhance the life of a person who's already reasonably happy, but it can't appreciably alter the outlook of someone who is essentially unhappy – it can only help to effect positive changes that my help.

In a small way, for some people, splashing out on a new outfit, spending on loved ones or investing money in a particular project does bring a certain kind of happiness, but it's of a more transient kind and isn't the same as deep contentment. The pleasure from a shopping spree is usually more about frivolity and indulgence than lasting happiness, and it can be the elation that comes from bagging a bargain or taking home a treat that makes spending feel particularly enjoyable. It might be worth putting aside a little cash in the run-up to the seasonal sales and treating yourself to something you wouldn't normally splash out on, for a little injection of pleasure.

Exercise 42

WORK OUT YOUR VALUES

We'll take a look at your current financial status and how you might improve it later in the chapter. First, though, we need to establish where materialistic things come on your priority list. Take a look at these two lists of happiness criteria and give each criterion a priority score of between 1 and 5, with 1 being low priority and 5 being the highest.

List A

▶ Enjoying good health   _____

▶ Watching my children develop   _____

▶ Spending time outdoors   _____

▶ Feeling appreciated by friends and family   _____

▶ Having a job that's rewarding   _____

▶ Finding time just for me   _____

▶ Loving and being loved   _____

▶ Feeling spiritually fulfilled   _____

▶ Taking up new challenges   _____

▶ Feeling generally in touch with nature   _____

     Total: _____

List B

- ▶ Buying a new car _____
- ▶ Earning good money _____
- ▶ Living in a big house _____
- ▶ Having regular holidays abroad _____
- ▶ Going on a spending spree _____
- ▶ Eating out at weekends _____
- ▶ Indulging friends and family _____
- ▶ Owning valuable jewellery _____
- ▶ Having the latest technology _____
- ▶ Knowing there's a lump sum in the bank _____

Total: _____

Add up the scores for each list. It's an interesting exercise as it can help you to see more clearly just what brings you the most happiness. If you scored list A higher overall, your priorities are more to do with things money can't buy than materialism. This in itself is quite self-affirming and means that you're more likely to be able to increase your experiences of these criteria as cost won't be a factor. You just need to organize your time a little better in order to free yourself up for more 'list A' activities. If list B comes out with a higher score overall, it seems as if you prize materialistic things more highly than more ethereal experiences – or perhaps you're not including the experiences on list A in your life often enough to score them highly. Some people do need more creature comforts than others, but if you analyse your lists further, are there some things on list A that are equally important to you as some of the things on list B? Could you focus more on increasing the time you spend on these, and work on giving lower priority to things that are both costly and dispensable? This could have a significant impact on your level of general contentment, especially in these times of financial uncertainty and relative insecurity.

→ For richer, for poorer?

'They say it is better to be poor and happy than rich and miserable, but how about a compromise like moderately rich and just moody?'

Diana, Princess of Wales

OK, the above quote was given tongue-in-cheek, but it does give rise to the question of how much money is enough? This often differs greatly from person to person and family to family. For the bloke down the pub, being able to afford an annual season ticket to follow his football team might well be a pleasure that lasts throughout the season, and that and a few pints are all he needs to spend on, in addition to his regular outgoings; for the next-door neighbours, what brings happiness could be the knowledge that there's a few thousand in the bank in case of a crisis. Some people are able to live hand-to-mouth without seeming to have a care in the world (although that may be a bit of a veneer in these straitened times); while others fret about spending on things they can actually comfortably afford. For some, there is never enough money to make ends meet, and the resulting anxiety can 'cancel out' other reasons for happiness.

Having expendable income doesn't necessarily make for happiness, though. You might be surprised to learn that children, for example, have recently been shown to prefer quality family leisure time to the latest gizmos and gadgets. This was one of a number of findings from a survey carried out by market research agency Opinion Matters. A few years ago UNICEF ranked the UK's children bottom of a league table for wellbeing. It then carried out a survey of children in Sweden, Spain and the UK (the other two countries being selected respectively as relatively equal and unequal to the UK). The researchers were told repeatedly by the kids that their happiness was dependent on having time with family and friends and having plenty to do outdoors, rather than on the materialistic things their parents were providing to make up for a lack of one-to-one attention. So how about we stop spoiling our children with 'things', switch off the TV and spend some quality time together as a family? If we do, it may be that this next generation will find themselves happier as adults than previous generations – and we'll save money into the bargain.

Here's another thought, and one that's backed up by research: having money and not using it is almost as likely to result in unhappiness as not having it in the first place – with the exception that some people do undoubtedly feel more secure knowing they have a 'buffer' should things take a turn for the worse. Analysing the results of a Social Trends survey carried out by the Office for National Statistics between 1987 and 2006 – which found that British families were healthier and twice as well off by the end of the survey as they were at the beginning, but no happier – British philosopher A. C. Grayling observed that people's expectations, aspirations and lifestyle are raised as our wealth increases, because we are always striving for more. He also commented that money only brings true happiness if it's used to fund pursuits that make us more enriched as people, saying: 'If you would like to know how rich a person is, you need to ask not how much money he has, but how much he has spent.' Perhaps it's just part of the human condition to be constantly striving to accumulate more money, material possessions and status symbols.

Are you happier spending, saving or doing a bit of both? And does your current situation and behaviour reflect this? It's interesting to know what motivates different attitudes towards accumulating or disposing of cash.

Some of the answers for why some people hoard money and yet, for others, it burns a hole in the pocket, can be found by measuring brain activity. Exploring the difference in behaviour between two groups of people he labelled 'tightwads' or 'spendthrifts', George Loewenstein, a professor of economics and psychology at Carnegie Mellon University, USA, says: 'Tightwads spend less than they should.' Talking to US online magazine LiveScience, he continues: 'They recognize that they should be spending more for their own wellbeing. The spendthrifts are the opposite. They spend more than they should spend by their own self-definition.'

Loewenstein and his team used functional magnetic resonance imaging (fMRI) to try and identify what happens in the brain when we think about spending. The technique monitors blood flow to areas in the brain activated when performing a task. The research showed that the reaction in the brain is very different when people look at something desirable from when they look at the price tag. In both groups, the area of the brain concerned with desirability became activated when they looked at the desired object. However, in the 'tightwads', the regions of the brain that register disgust and pain became activated when they contemplated price and spending, whereas in the 'spendthrifts', these regions didn't register. Hopefully your pattern of spending and saving is more moderate than either of these groups. Loewenstein does have some advice, however, to modify the extreme behaviours of both, advocating that 'tightwads' experiment with multiple bank accounts, for example dedicating one to saving and another to spending. 'Spendthrifts' on the other hand should avoid credit cards and set themselves weekly budgets.

Exercise 43

ARE YOU A 'SPENDTHRIFT' OR A 'TIGHTWAD'?

Now let's see what your spending/saving behaviour is really like. Answer the following questions to reveal which stereotype you more closely resemble.

1 In a restaurant with friends, you usually:

   a. Pick up the bill yourself.

   b. Split it 50/50 regardless of what everyone had.

   c. Break the bill down to the penny so that everyone pays for exactly what they had and no more.

2 You're going to friends for dinner. What do you take?

   a. A bottle of wine, flowers and chocolates.

   b. A bottle of wine, flowers OR chocolates.

   c. Nothing. They'll come to us next time, so it'll all work out equally.

3 In a supermarket, what's your thinking about BOGOFs (Buy One, Get One Free)?

   a. I only buy them if I know I can use the extra products up before the expiry date.

   b. I buy them if the items were on my shopping list in any case.

   c. I buy as many as I can, substituting them for the things I'd originally wanted if necessary.

4 What's your approach to holidays?

   a. I book ahead to get the nicest accommodation.

   b. I keep checking for bargains, but make sure I book in plenty of time.

   c. I only book if I can get a very special deal; otherwise, I don't bother with holidays.

5 **How often do you treat yourself to something a bit frivolous?**

    a. Probably two or three times a month.

    b. Once every few months or so.

    c. Virtually never: if it's frivolous I can do without it.

6 **If you found a substantial amount of money in the street, what would you do with it?**

    a. Hand it in to the police station and hope whoever lost it manages to claim it.

    b. Put it into a charity box.

    c. Take it home: there's no way of knowing who it belonged to anyway.

7 **When you're entertaining, what's your approach to food?**

    a. I lay on everything and wouldn't expect any contribution.

    b. I ask guests to bring a starter or pudding.

    c. I tend to do 'pot luck' lunches, with everyone bringing something.

8 **If you won the Lottery, what would you do?**

    a. Share the good fortune with friends, family and charities.

    b. Help the family, pay off any debts, clear the mortgage and invest the rest.

    c. Say nothing, put the money away and carry on as normal.

9 What's your attitude to present-giving?

  a. I love to give presents for all occasions and sometimes spontaneously.

  b. I buy for friends and family at Christmas and on birthdays.

  c. I don't believe in present-giving: it's a waste of money.

10 When faced with a charity collector, what do you do?

  a. I give whatever I can in addition to donating regularly to chosen charities.

  b. I make regular donations to selected charities, but don't donate to street collectors.

  c. I don't give to charities – they have enough other people donating already.

Mostly 'a': You are certainly generous and could be thought of by some as a bit of a spendthrift. As long as you have enough resources to cope with emergencies and your longer term future, there's no harm in spending. Sometimes, though, excessive spending can be a response to stress or unhappiness. The things you buy – especially if they are unnecessary or are duplicates of what you already have – will probably not bring you happiness except in the short term. Try to think of other ways of finding gratification: refer back to list A in the previous exercise for ideas.

Mostly 'b': You seem to have a well-balanced attitude to spending and don't try to fill any gaps in your life with material things, but you do spend for pleasure if you consider it to be of value. Other people appreciate your generosity but you also derive pleasure from giving. By ensuring that you have enough money put away to give you the best chance of security, you're being responsible. Materialism isn't part of your fibre any more than it needs to be.

Mostly 'c': Some would describe you as 'careful with money'; others as a 'tightwad'. Whilst it's true that we, as a nation, are living in straitened times financially, you may be restricting your own happiness by being as parsimonious with yourself as you are. OK, others might find your attitude towards money a bit restricting – especially if it means you don't join in with events and activities that, whilst they would cost you, would bring you all together – but it's not other people that matter most here. See if you can let go of the purse strings a little bit – just enough to indulge yourself now and then. You don't have to go wildly over the top: it might just be something small that you'd usually deny yourself, like stopping for a coffee during a big shopping trip. If it makes you feel more relaxed, how about reviewing your weekly or monthly budget and juggling things around so that you can find some extra spending money whilst still maintaining control over how much you spend? You may feel it's your responsibility to plough every penny you have into your kids' futures, but you also have a responsibility to show them how to really live and enjoy life – and to teach them that it's OK to treat yourself with your hard-earned cash. In fact, it's more than OK: it's expected, normal behaviour.

→ ## To have or have not?

'Wealth consists not in having great possessions, but in having few wants.'

Epictetus, Greek philosopher

Possessions can bring their own happiness, particularly if they spark a certain happy memory or were once the property of a loved one. This isn't so much to do with materialism, though: it's more to do with sentimentality, and that's a bittersweet emotion for most of us. Happiness, when tinged with sadness, is often particularly poignant. Some possessions have special value, too, if we've worked hard to get them, or if we appreciate them often. Clutter, on the other hand, can cause us more anxiety than happiness. The above quote by Epictetus illustrates that happiness is more likely to come from *not* needing or coveting 'things', but from personal fulfilment and inner contentment. Clearing unnecessary or unwanted clutter from our lives can give us a better appreciation of what's left, and the satisfaction of knowing that we've chosen to keep only things of real value to us. Who doesn't derive a sense of real satisfaction from clearing out a cupboard or reorganizing a space in the home, creating a sense of clarity, order and spaciousness? Accumulating stuff – whether possessions or money – also sets us up for a fall if we find ourselves in a position where we lose them. It may be better to have loved and lost than never to have loved at all (Alfred Lord Tennyson), but according to many research studies, it may very well be better never to have acquired wealth than to have acquired it then lost it. A US survey, funded by The Bill and Melinda Gates Foundation, spoke to 160 households, of which 120 had at least $25 million in assets, and found that many were, in fact, miserable. With wealth comes the fear of losing it; or of being in a more privileged position than our peers, and therefore feeling less comfortable with complaining about other aspects of our lives and more open to criticism; and of raising children who feel they're automatically entitled to money and possessions without necessarily earning the right.

Some of us who find it hard to relinquish possessions that are no longer of any use to us might be filling an emotional gap with material things. It's not uncommon for the bereaved to surround themselves with more and more 'stuff' in order to feel secure. Some individuals find it understandably hard to clear out their loved one's clothing and personal effects, but others may even begin to hoard things that aren't necessarily either useful or sanitary: they can find it hard to throw out newspapers, packaging and even food that's past its best, as if holding on to things may somehow fill the gaping hole created by grief. This sort of behaviour tends to respond well to professional bereavement counselling. Less extreme 'holding-on' tendencies usually lessen with the passing of time, especially as the memory of the lost person becomes stronger than the pull of their possessions.

Exercise 44

DE-CLUTTER TO SEE MORE CLEARLY

Draw a rough floor plan of your house on a sheet of A4 paper. Assign at least a part of each main room to be de-cluttered, and mark a target date for achieving it (being realistic and setting achievable goals!) Pin the plan up somewhere prominent and work through room by room, sticking as closely to your individual deadlines as you can. Sort things into four categories: keep, bin, recycle or give to charity. Be a bit ruthless, but if there's anything that genuinely makes you hesitate for more than a couple of minutes, put it aside and come back to it. Later, analyse your attachment to these pieces and examine whether relinquishing them would really have any impact on the memories they help to evoke. Perhaps you could group things together and photograph them for posterity. Try to focus on the enjoyment or practical use these items could bring others and then select one or two to treasures and try to let the rest go. Don't feel obliged to keep stuff from other people that doesn't mean a great deal to you. A good de-clutter not only lifts the spirits but creates a more comfy living space and makes way for a few new possessions.

....

→ # Money management

'I have enough money to last me the rest of my life, unless I buy something.'

Jackie Mason, US comedian

If there's one issue that crops up time and again amongst rowing couples, it's money. According to an annual survey into divorce conducted by UK accountancy firm Grant Thornton, 5 per cent of divorces currently cite money as the reason for the split. The problems can be varied: in some couples, one partner takes responsibility for the finances; in others both partners are equally involved; in some, both are equally irresponsible. Disharmony can occur when one or other person is irresponsible with jointly earned cash; where one partner is a control freak over the coffers or when both partners adopt the mindset 'Spend it while you've got it' and either jointly shun responsibility or else blame each other. It's no use trying to change people, though: the best way forward is to play to what motivates them. Say, for example, you are an incorrigible spendthrift, but being short of cash makes you unhappy. It may help you to spend little and often on small frivolities and put some money aside for a more gratifying purchase (earmark a date in the diary as a target for reaching the required amount). Once your purchase is made, start again with another goal, so that you'll only ever lay out large amounts of money when you've saved it up. This way, you're not curbing your basic tendency to want to spend, but you're channelling it in a more constructive way.

You can't expect to change your partner greatly, either, so if they have, for example, a controlling side when it comes to finances, however much it pains you, sit down together and work out exactly what's needed to cover your monthly outgoings; how much you're jointly bringing in; how much you both agree to save or invest, and how much is left for spending. Playing to their cautious side will show you're taking things seriously and may encourage them to splash out on the occasional treat with the left-over cash.

You can apply these principles to yourself and/or your partner, regardless of your particular shortcomings: play to your own strengths, reward yourself where appropriate and bask in the enjoyment of having tackled your finances head on and taken control.

Exercise 45

WEIGH UP YOUR CASH FLOW

Complete the table to find out whether you're living beyond your means. Some rows are left blank for you to add any other outgoings you may have.

Joint total monthly income:_____

Outgoings (NB Where an outgoing is annual, such as car tax or TV licence, divide by 12 to find the monthly amount.)	Amount
Mortgage/rent	
Utility bills (phone/energy/internet services/water rates)	
Council tax	
Car tax and insurance	
Other insurances	
Childcare	
Pension contribution	
TV licence	
Petrol	

Outgoings (NB Where an outgoing is annual, such as car tax or TV licence, divide by 12 to find the monthly amount.)	Amount
Commuting costs	
Overdraft charges (if applicable)	
Food and drink	
Charitable donations	
Credit card repayments	
Loan repayments	
Savings/investments	
Medical insurance	
Clothing and grooming	

Outgoings (NB Where an outgoing is annual, such as car tax or TV licence, divide by 12 to find the monthly amount.)	Amount
Leisure (eating out/pub/day trips/sports)	
Pet insurance/costs	
Total outgoings:	

If you have more outgoings than income per month, discuss things you could trim back on. It might also be worth considering long-term saving options like installing a more energy-efficient boiler or insulating your loft. If, on the other hand, you have money left over each month, even after saving some, why not plan a couple of weekends away that you can both look forward to? Or treat yourselves to something you would normally consider extravagant? However you spend it, spend it on something that brings you pleasure. Meantime, see how many other money-saving ideas you can come up with. There are some great websites that can help you do this, including www.moneysavingexpert.com and www.talkmoneyblog.co.uk.

Summary

Hopefully this chapter has revealed a lot about your attitude to materialism and finances that you were perhaps previously unaware of: you may have had your views firmly entrenched from childhood, either because of your own parents' way of managing things or because you come from a background where money was in short supply. You'll have brought into sharp focus what is really important to you materially and examined whether or not it can really bring you happiness or is more of a crutch. Yes, being financially stable can bring great security, but in this current climate where money is less valuable than ever before, it may be time to turn to less tangible things for fulfilment. Hopefully you'll have taught yourself ways of managing your resources better, to take some of the stress out of making ends meet; you'll have discovered your personal spending style and got an insight into what drives you, along with ideas for possible changes in attitude that could benefit you – all of which should help you to feel more contented and happy with your situation.

So what's next for the emotional microscope? We're going to look at lifestyles and how the choices you make and the way you prioritize your time can have a big impact on your happiness levels.

My happiness journal

This space is for jotting down any thoughts, feelings or ideas you might have at this stage – it is purely optional.

→ **My thoughts on happiness at this moment**

_____

_____

_____

_____

_____

_____

_____

_____

_____

_____

_____

_____

_____

_____

_____

_____

_____

_____

_____

_____

→ My ideas for change

Happiness and lifestyles

'Happiness doesn't come as a result of getting something we don't have, but rather of recognizing and appreciating what we do have.'

Frederick Koenig, German inventor

Are men or women generally happier? Have a think about your own relationships with men and women – both in your family and outside – and you'll probably draw your own conclusions. But have you analysed the various factors and life stages for both genders that could influence overall happiness? Research studies have found that both sexes tend to be at their happiest – as well as at their lowest – at conflicting points in their lives. One study, detailed below, suggests that women feel generally more contented than men up to the age of 48, when happiness levels apparently start to slide, and men feel at their least happy in their twenties, when the majority of them are single, but overtake women in the happiness stakes at age 48. Depending on your age, you may already agree or disagree with this – or you may be just starting out in life or find yourself in your thirties or early forties and not sure how to measure your happiness.

→ Ages and stages

'Youth would be an ideal state if it came a little later in life.'

Herbert Henry Asquith, former UK Prime Minister

The key to the findings, from Cambridge University researcher Anke Plagnol, who worked with Richard Easterlin, an economist from the University of Southern California, seems to hang on changes to earnings and family life. Apparently, women are more satisfied overall than their male counterparts when they first embark on adult life, feeling quite happy with their general situation, earnings and achievement, whereas young men – even those on an equal footing – have higher financial expectations, which leaves them feeling dissatisfied.

Longer-term, though, women are less likely to feel they have met all their goals, which is perhaps down to the years spent parenting and missing out on career progression and independence. By age 41, the study suggests, men are financially more contented than women; and at age 48, they take over from women in terms of greater happiness. The study also reveals that in later life, because women tend to live longer than men, they are more likely to face widowhood, which increases anxiety levels, whereas men are more likely to have their partners with them into their own old age. And at age 64, a man's satisfaction with his family circumstances tends to overtake a woman's once and for all.

Whatever your age, it can help to stop and reflect on your present happiness compared with past contentment. Have certain factors, perhaps – especially financial stability, job satisfaction and personal relationships – changed, either for better or worse, since new adulthood? Sometimes just recognizing and acknowledging which changes have influenced our sense of wellbeing can be helpful in getting things into perspective. It can sometimes help to reflect on what does bring you a sense of satisfaction and fulfilment at this stage in your life, and to focus on these aspects as often as possible. They could include having achieved academically or in a vocational sense; having a job you enjoy; having created a beautiful home or garden or having raised a family – or any greater or smaller aspects that make you proud.

Exercise 46

MAKE A MAP OF YOUR LIFE

Firstly, make a mental note of how happy you are today on a scale of one to ten. Now take a large sheet of paper and a pen. Starting at point 'A', which will represent your earliest meaningful memories – perhaps around the time of starting school – start to recall what brought you overall happiness and what brought you unhappiness and write these memories down under the headings 'positive' and 'negative'. Move on to the next significant point, labelling it 'B' – it might be moving up to high school or going to college, for example – and repeat the exercise. Do this, working from A–Z (although you probably won't find 26 life stages to analyse, no matter what your age, so stop when you feel your map is complete). Include all the significant periods in your life. Depending on your age and personal circumstances, these might include your first romantic relationship; your first experience of living independently; your first foray into the working world; any periods of time when you have not been in a relationship; your life since getting married or making a long-term commitment; pregnancy and becoming a parent; living with a much-loved pet; giving up or returning to work; best and worst holidays; best and worst Christmases; bereavements – the list will depend entirely on how significant various life events have been to you personally. This part of the exercise can be done over several days if it's very time-consuming. You can make the map as elaborate as you like, perhaps by adding photos or other significant memorabilia.

Now go back to point 'A' and mentally travel along your map, stopping at each point to see if you could replicate in your present life stage any of the happiness you experienced back then, or whether you have moved on from any or all of the experiences that made you unhappy. Try to relive the pleasant memories and accept, but dismiss the unpleasant ones: they belong in the past and need have no further influence on your life today. When you come to the end of the exercise, note again how happy you are from one to ten. Hopefully you'll have raised your happiness levels. You can revisit your map whenever you're feeling low.

→ Working or staying home?

'Far and away the best prize that life has to offer is the chance to work hard at work worth doing.'

Theodore Roosevelt, 26th president of the USA

Some of us do paid work, some of us don't. For some of us it's a choice, for others it isn't. When it comes to your happiness – or otherwise – your personal working circumstances and how much control you have over them are likely to be hugely influential. But even if you're able to dictate your own terms, it doesn't necessarily mean you're contented. Perhaps, for instance, you choose to work for the social interaction, but the job you do doesn't fulfil you, or piles on way too much pressure. Or maybe you've chosen to stay at home to enable someone more in need of the money to gain employment, but find yourself isolated and discontented. Perhaps the answer – if you're lucky enough to be in a position to choose – is to have the best of both worlds by working part-time in a job that's less demanding. Or to take a voluntary position so that you get all the benefits of working with others, but aren't depriving anyone more in need of an income. For most of us, though, work is a necessity and we don't have the luxury of choice.

If you're a parent, the conundrum becomes ever more complicated. Are you a stay-at-home, full-time parent whose whole life seems to be taken up with chores and childcare? The downsides are that you may be suffering from a loss of identity; a feeling that you've lost touch with working life; a drop in self-esteem, and guilt that you're not contributing financially to the family income.

There are enviable aspects to your situation, though, even if it doesn't feel like it at the moment: you're there for your children all the time, bringing them up and giving them the benefit of your love and wisdom; you're unlikely to miss their first milestone achievements; you can feel secure in the knowledge that they're getting the very best care – and that money couldn't buy better (as long as you're coping and getting a sense of fulfilment out of the arrangement). You're there for your partner, if you have one, at the end of each day; you don't have to answer to anyone or work to someone else's agenda (with the possible exception of your child's!) Focus on these positives every day and remember: one day, when you're not looking and your children have outgrown the need for you to be there all day, things can and will change if you let them.

Perhaps you are that parent whose children have recently become independent enough that you don't need you to be indoors, waiting for them to come home from school, and you're feeling a bit lost and redundant. A whole new world of opportunities could open up for you if you keep your eyes open: perhaps you feel like retraining or gaining a degree to widen your scope for employment? Maybe you could look into becoming a childminder in your own home? If you don't need to return to paid employment, you could get involved with voluntary work – anything from helping out in a charity shop to prison visiting or training to become a tour guide for the National Trust. If your family has left home and you find yourself at a loose end but at the wrong end of the age scale for re-employment, perhaps you could start a social circle of local women all in your position? It's simple enough to find them via local networking websites. You could organize walks, lunches out, coffee mornings at each other's houses, book clubs, film nights or whatever takes your fancy. Or check out your local leisure centre to see if there are daytime classes you might enjoy that'll put you in touch with others and will have the added bonus of increasing your fitness levels.

Working parents, especially mums, can feel enormously guilty about placing their kids into someone else's care for such a large proportion of time – even if that person is a friend or family member – and can feel they're not doing a good enough job either at work or at home. The twin demands of work and parenthood can make you feel as if you're being pulled in both directions yet not excelling at either. But whether you need to work for money or because you can't cope with the idea of being a full-time parent, there's no need to feel guilty. If you're working through necessity, the choice is out of your hands, unless you and your partner can find a way round your need to earn money. You should congratulate yourself on helping provide for your family. If you're doing it for your own sanity, that's just as good a reason: a happier, more fulfilled mum or dad will inevitably be a happier parent – and that can only be a good thing. In these times where every penny counts, it's a positive thing to reinforce to children that working is an ethically sound and responsible thing to do if you can.

Exercise 47

PROS AND CONS TO CONSIDER

Take the following quiz to clarify how happy or otherwise you are with your current situation.

1 How often do you wish you could change your life?

    a. Constantly – the thought's never far from my mind.

    b. Sometimes – perhaps every few weeks or months.

    c. Hardly ever – and even then it's usually a knee-jerk response to a temporary blip.

2 How happy you are with the amount of time you spend at home?

    a. I need to change the amount of time I'm at home for my own mental wellbeing.

    b. It would be nice to adjust the balance a bit sometimes.

    c. I think I've got it about right most of the time.

3 Have you got an idea of what it is you'd do differently?

    a. Yes, I've got a new direction in mind, if only it was achievable.

b. I get inspired by other people, but never really follow the ideas up.

c. No. I've never got that far with my thinking.

4 Do finances play a big part in your current situation?

a. Without a doubt – the need for money has taken away my choices.

b. Up to a point – we could perhaps manage with a bit less.

c. No – I'm able to choose whether or not I work.

5 How happy are you with your input as a parent?

a. I need to be there more for my kids – it feels like someone else is bringing them up.

b. They seem well adjusted and happy – it's just that I'd prefer to spend more time with them.

c. I think we all benefit from the arrangement as it stands.

If you answered mostly 'a', it's time to sit down and work out how you can change your life for the better. You might have to think laterally: if you need to find work, do you have transferable skills that aren't immediately obvious? Being a parent, for instance, demands that you have to be a great organizer; a good listener; a brilliant communicator; a problem solver and resourceful in every way. Why not register with some agencies, listing these qualities on your CV? If, on the other hand, you are working more than you'd like, could you organize to go part-time, job share or work from home sometimes?

Could you do flexi hours? Are you in a position to ask for a pay increase?

If you answered mostly 'b', you seem fairly contented overall, but there's probably room for small adjustments that would make life better all round. Think along the lines of the mostly 'a' advice, but on a smaller scale. If you're a full-time mum, for instance, could you start up a mums-and-babies coffee morning group for times when you're lonely or isolated? If you work, could you alternate doing the school run with your partner, then start work earlier and leave earlier? If you don't have children, could you work more flexibly or retrain within your company with a view to switching role?

If you answered mostly 'c', it seems as if you've got it all worked out on the work/life balance front. Don't forget to build in 'me' time whenever you can: we all have more to give to our partners and children in terms of love and attention, but only if we have opportunities to replenish these levels within ourselves with a bit of rest, relaxation and pampering.

→ All in the genes?

'I've learned from experience that the greater part of our happiness or misery depends on our dispositions and not on our circumstances.'

Martha Washington, wife of George Washington, first president of the USA

There appears to be a genetic link that explains why some people are naturally more optimistic and have a sunnier outlook than others – although, according to the researchers who made this discovery, that doesn't mean that those without the 'happy' gene are condemned to a life of abject misery: it's just that some people are more predisposed to cheeriness, so they have something of a head start when it comes to tackling life's trials.

A study of more than 2,500 Americans by Jan-Emmanuel De Neve, a researcher at the London School of Economics and Political Science, which was published in 2011, found that individuals born with two long versions of gene 5-HTT – one from each parent – were happier overall than those born with two short versions. Even one long version and one short seemed to raise general levels of satisfaction with life. Conversely, people with two short versions are more prone to depression in response to stress.

All of this is interesting, to say the least, but where does it leave us? Well, as most of us will probably never be genetically tested to find out whether or not we possess the longer or shorter version of gene 5-HTT, it leaves us nowhere other than a little more enlightened about the mechanics of happiness. What it does enable us to do, though, is stop beating ourselves up if we worry that we're less optimistic than we could be, or that others see us as the harbinger of gloom and doom. It's no excuse for being deliberately miserable – of course not! – but it may give us some clues as to why we may not naturally be the person whose glass is permanently half full rather than half empty. Acceptance of ourselves for who we really are, as long as we're striving for our own greater happiness and the happiness of those around us, can be very helpful in itself and enables us to forgive or overlook our own limitations.

→ Teach others to accept you as you are

'Human beings, like plants, grow in the soil of acceptance, not in the atmosphere of rejection.'

John Powell, British composer

A common response amongst those of us who don't feel quite 'good enough' is to bend over backwards to gain other people's acceptance and approval. If you've long had the habit of being a bit of a 'yes' person, perhaps it's time for a subtle shift in attitude. You'll increase your feelings of self-worth and esteem no end if you start to put yourself first more often. It's not selfish – it's an important part of showing yourself and others that you respect yourself as much as other people. Don't try to temper your personality to fit in better with friends and family: let your inner spirit shine through – who knows, you might really surprise people, and that might not necessarily be a bad thing. Being yourself doesn't mean paying no regard to the opinions and attitudes of other people and bludgeoning your way through life: you can pay attention to other people's views and choose either to accept them or put them aside, and you can treat yourself in the same way.

Exercise 48

REFLECT BEFORE YOU REACT

Next time someone who's important to you criticizes your behaviour, rather than reacting straightaway, ask them to explain how it has affected them (unless, of course, it's obvious) and why and how they think you should change. You now need to time to contemplate what you've heard, so say 'I'll certainly give that some thought'. This way, you've acknowledged the message and agreed to think it over – but, crucially, you haven't submitted to that person's opinion without question or admitted to any failings. Now take some time consider whether or not you feel there was genuine cause for criticism and whether a change in your behaviour would be of all-round benefit. If so, try to make a change. If you agree with a criticism about a long-held behaviour or attitude of yours, it'll probably take time for you to break the habit, so point out that you're working on it and ask your critic to bear with you. Depending on the circumstances, you may even find it helpful to ask them to check you whenever you repeat the offending behaviour. If on the other hand you don't agree with your critic, explain that you're happy with your behaviour and suggest politely that the other person takes a little time to think about accepting individual differences. Practise this technique often until you're more comfortable in your own skin.

Summary

Sometimes we can get stuck with the thought that our present lifestyle is the only choice we have, especially if we're at a stage in our lives where responsibility weighs heavily, but hopefully you've taught yourself in this last chapter that there are possibilities for making changes, whatever your current circumstances. By charting your life in terms of different lifestyles at different ages and stages, you'll have identified what has made you happiest, and have begun to work out how you can bring some of that same happiness into your current situation. You'll have discovered things about your behaviour towards other people as well, and learned that some of it is innate to your character, and that rather than feeling guilty and trying to conform to others' ideals it's OK to stand firm and assert yourself for who you are. You'll also have taught yourself that in some cases a bit of self-examination can be useful in your ongoing interactions with others, and that every lifestyle is about give and take.

Where to next?

In Chapter 9 we'll be seeking to discover who you really want to be: perhaps you felt more 'alive' in a previous period of your life; maybe you feel you've lost your sense of individuality since becoming a partner or parent; perhaps your job is stifling your true personality. The aim is for you to feel happy with who you are today, whether this means accepting that you have changed; journeying back in time to retrieve some aspects of a previous 'you' or adopting some of the most positive influences of your favourite role models.

My happiness journal

This space is for jotting down any thoughts, feelings or ideas you might have at this stage – it is purely optional.

→ **My thoughts on happiness at this moment**

_____

_____

_____

_____

_____

_____

_____

_____

_____

_____

_____

_____

_____

_____

_____

_____

_____

_____

→ **My ideas for change**

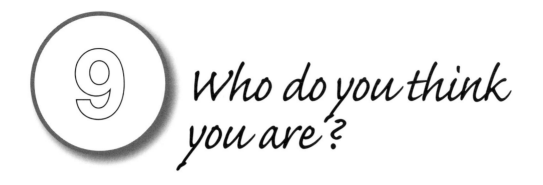

Who do you think you are?

'The person who is most versatile has more going for him than a guy who does just one thing.'

Terence Newman, American footballer

We lead multi-faceted lives, many of us performing multiple roles. Those of us who are parents take on perhaps the most diverse roles: we're unqualified (in some cases) teachers, nurses, counsellors, dietitians and play therapists. In addition, along with our childless friends, we're likely to be partners, colleagues, bosses, friends and relatives. Some of us feel more defined by one or more of these roles than by any of the others, whereas some of us are equally comfortable with any or all.

Along with multiple roles, many of us have more than one persona: there's who we are at work; who we are with our friends; who we are with our other halves, our parents, our kids. Maybe you think you're the same with everyone, regardless of who you're with – but stop and think: do you *really* speak to your partner or workmates in the same way you speak to your children? Would you necessarily discuss the same topics with your mum that you'd chat to your mates about? What about the way you communicate with your partner? Does that equate to your conversations with other people? When you analyse it, probably not.

Have you ever taken the time to think which of your roles makes you happiest and most fulfilled? Or which 'you' feels the most natural? Do you get the best feedback from your partner, your child or your friends? Are you comfortable with the conversations you have with your boss and colleagues? Do you enjoy talking to strangers? Are you ever uncomfortable with your family or your partner's?

The point isn't to try and change the way you behave or communicate in certain situations, or to eliminate completely any uncomfortable situations from your daily routine – it's to help you focus on which roles and situations bring you the most enjoyment and to encourage you to explore ways of increasing the amount of time you spend doing these.

Exercise 49

FIND THE FEEL-GOOD FACTORS

Take time to consider the following statements and tick 'Always', 'Sometimes', 'Never' (choosing the option that's nearest to your true feelings generally).

→ *I look forward to talking with my children*
  Always ❏ Sometimes ❏ Never ❏

→ *I love chatting with my partner*
  Always ❏ Sometimes ❏ Never ❏

→ *Being a daughter/sister/other relative is fulfilling*
  Always ❏ Sometimes ❏ Never ❏

→ *I feel valued as an employee*
  Always ❏ Sometimes ❏ Never ❏

→ *I get on well with my colleagues*
  Always ❏ Sometimes ❏ Never ❏

→*I like being with other adults*
Always ❏   Sometimes ❏   Never ❏

→*I enjoy being around lots of children*
Always ❏   Sometimes ❏   Never ❏

→*I love the interaction I have with friends*
Always ❏   Sometimes ❏   Never ❏

→*I like it when strangers talk to me*
Always ❏   Sometimes ❏   Never ❏

→*I like being introduced to new people*
Always ❏   Sometimes ❏   Never ❏

Now look at where the most 'Always' ticks are. Could you include more contact with these people than you have currently? Say you've ticked 'Always' next to 'I love chatting with my partner', and yet you don't find enough opportunities for conversations that progress much beyond 'How was your day?' or 'Do you want a cup of tea to take up to bed?': perhaps you could make a conscious change in the way your evenings run so that there's a window of time for you to catch up with each other. Could the kids be amused by a short DVD and the evening meal put back by 15 minutes? Maybe you could eat that bit earlier and use the extra time for a one-to-one conversation after the children are in bed? If you don't have children, it may be that you're not giving each other priority, possibly out of habit. If you tend to be preoccupied with social networking sites, TV or other distractions, could you introduce a house rule that there should be an hour per day when everything is put aside – say at dinner time? It's really easy to fall into habits that exclude partners, especially if you've been together a long time, you work different hours or your relationship has turned a bit stale. In these circumstances, you might even find it a challenge to think of things to talk about at first during your new-found 'couple time', but as long as you make a concerted effort (perhaps by bringing up a news topic you both have views about or by both reading the same book, then having a discussion about it) it'll come more naturally as time goes by. Remember, you've already earmarked chats with your partner as one of the things you most cherish, so it'll be worth a period of awkwardness to get more special time together.

If, on the other hand, you've ticked the 'Always' box next to 'I get on well with my colleagues', perhaps you could spend a little more time with them? A lot of us – particularly part-time workers and/or full-time parents – complain of spending too little time away from the family and in the company of other 'grown-ups'. If you find yourself tied to the house more than you'd like, could you perhaps organize some regular lunches with colleagues? Or see if there are meetings it would be beneficial for you to attend? Perhaps you could pitch the idea of a monthly social evening together? It's empowering and affirming to spend time with people you like and respect and who – more importantly – like and respect you back. Spending time in the company of others who make us feel good, and who allow us to be ourselves as individuals is a great self-esteem booster. You might also find you become inspired to take on new challenges, undergo some training or otherwise change your working life as a result of networking in this way.

Whichever boxes you've ticked, see if you can apply the above examples to help you spend more time being with people whose company you most appreciate – and who appreciate you, too.

→ Be who you want to be

'Dream what you want to dream; go where you want to go; be what you want to be, because you have only one life and one chance to do all the things you want to do.'

Author unknown

Are you happy that you're the person you want to be, both in terms of your outlook and your life circumstances? It may be that right now you're very involved with being a parent but that you'd like to find more time for yourself as an individual, or perhaps you're longing for a family, but the timing isn't right. Maybe you're perfectly happy channelling your energies into your career, or perhaps you feel that your job is defining you too much and you'd like to break away. In order to feel fulfilled and contented, we need to understand who we really want to be.

Exercise 50

WHO'S YOUR ROLE MODEL?

There's research that supports the idea that simply by mentally stepping into the persona of someone we admire, we feel more confident, assertive, even attractive. Most of us can remember specific role models from our pasts that we have aspired to imitate: yours might be a schoolteacher; a family friend; a favourite aunt; that cool neighbour from up the road; a friend's parent; your own parent… the list is endless. Think for a minute about who used to impress you most, and what it was about them you most admired. Now think whether you have any role models today. They could be an actor; an author; a TV presenter; a colleague or employer; a local shopkeeper; one of your children's teachers... again, the list is almost inexhaustible. Make a mental comparison between your role models then and now. Do they share similar traits or are they quite different? Are there elements of either or both that you'd like to emulate now? What's stopping you?

Just as we can laugh ourselves happy, even when we're disinclined to laugh at all, we can also begin to take on the attributes of people we look up to, the more we adopt their characteristics or mimic their personalities. Try it for yourself, but don't go too far: you're trying to emulate your role model, not *become* them. If the person you'd like to resemble is graceful of movement, for example, bring them into the forefront of your mind as you go about your daily jobs: lift and move objects the way they would; place things as they might; hold yourself as you've seen them hold themselves. Feel any different?

Exercise 51

WHAT DO I WANT TO CHANGE AND WHY?

Fill in the chart to help you to identify more clearly what you'd like to change and how it will benefit you. The first three rows have been filled in to give you ideas for the sorts of things you might want to include when you complete the table.

I want to be more...	I want to be less...	How change will benefit me
Assertive	Self-conscious	Raise my self-esteem
Involved with people	Isolated	Rekindle social skills
Graceful of movement	Clumsy	Improve my image

So now you know more about who you want to be, it's time to think about what action you can take to effect a change. Making changes isn't easy – and in some cases change will have to be put on hold while you move through an important phase of life, such as bringing up a family – but it could be the key to lasting happiness long term.

→ Plan for change

'Nobody can go back and start a new beginning, but anyone can start today and make a new ending.'

Maria Robinson, American writer

We're not talking about a complete personality transplant here, by the way – just a restoration to your true self, along with some of the positive traits you've picked up from mimicking your role model. Yes, it will involve making some changes, and change can be a scary prospect: many of us prefer to stick with what we know rather than break away, purely because of the fear of how much better or worse the outcome will be. Don't panic: these positive changes can be made in small steps. Firstly, if you really can't make any meaningful changes right now, accept the fact and embrace it: every situation has its pros and cons, so look at the positives for now, while continuing to plan for change at a later date. If you can see an opportunity to change things now so that you can be more the person you want to be, start to plan for that. If your job is stifling your true personality, for instance, make an effort to network with the sorts of people who are already in roles similar to one you feel would suit you better. Sign up to job alerts from agencies and newspapers specializing in your preferred career. If you've always dreamed of starting your own small business, do some extensive online research to get a better idea of whether this is a good route for you to follow. If you have a hobby that interests you more than your job, consider whether it's something you could turn into a business or a work opportunity. Put some feelers out: join some social networking sites or forums of people who are already living the life you want for yourself. See if anyone would agree to mentor you in a new role.

You may be sorted on the work front, but feel you've lost sight of your core personality – or perhaps frustration or a change in lifestyle or circumstances has changed your usual outlook. You may feel you're less optimistic than you used to be; more anxious; less carefree; more critical; less humorous. Ask yourself – or, if you're brave enough, other people – what may have changed you. Some people find that leaving university and finding themselves in the midst of the 'real world' changes them from happy-go-lucky individuals to anxious types, fretting about finding employment, getting on the property ladder and earning enough to provide for themselves longer term. Some people find that new parenthood alters their outlook in general: they may become more fearful about the outside world and what lies in wait for their children; or more serious about education and legislation. Others feel purposeless and unfulfilled after their children have grown up and left home. Some people allow their personalities to become overtaken by their partners' thoughts, politics and beliefs. Whatever your personal circumstances, if you feel you've changed there'll be an underlying reason, and once you've identified that, you can start to turn things around.

If, for example, you're suffering from 'empty nest syndrome' because your children have all left home, you could consider becoming involved in a local youth group to keep you in touch with young people. Or maybe you could start one up yourself in a church or village hall – somewhere that already has the necessary facilities and insurances? Perhaps you could think about becoming a career mentor: some local high schools might be running a voluntary mentoring scheme.

If you're fresh from uni, on the other hand, and feel you're carrying the troubles of the world on your shoulders, see if you can get in touch with other new graduates in your area and start a support group: it could mean just meeting up at the pub once a week or so to catch up with how you're all getting on, or it could be buddying up with someone in your efforts to find work. The idea is to try to find a solution to the downturn in your outlook that will help to restore your true personality, even though your circumstances may have changed.

Exercise 52

WRITE A PERSONAL CV

This is less about putting together a CV to present to prospective employers (although you may be able to use parts of it to rewrite your professional CV, too) and more about identifying your personal strengths and desires, weaknesses and dislikes. Here's a template you can use for starters: you might be inspired to add to it and create your own categories.

My strengths: (e.g. friendliness; empathy; dependability; organizational skills; deadline-driven; self-starter; generosity of time and material things; good listener)

My weaknesses: (e.g. not a great timekeeper; impulsiveness; intolerance of conflicting views; untidiness)

My loves: (e.g. open-air spaces; travel; company of others; free thinkers; holidays; reading; writing; drawing; cooking; time spent with family)

My dislikes: (e.g. early mornings; late nights; own company; crowded places; meeting strangers)

My aspirations: (e.g. a new job; new skills; to be more like old self; to be more like role model; to really enjoy life and set the same example to others)

Spend some time adding to your personal CV over a few days rather than trying to get it all down in one go. A bit of reflection might expand your input to give you a broader account of yourself. Ask a close friend or family member to go through it with you and give you honest feedback to add to your lists. Remember, this isn't for public release – it's a tool just for your private use. When you feel your CV is complete, see how well your current situation – at work, at home and socially – fulfils your strengths and loves, or how many of your weaknesses and dislikes it incorporates. This can be a useful tool in giving you clarity and helping you to consider possible changes for the better by finding more outlets for the things you really enjoy.

Summary

Well, that was quite a journey of self-discovery, and you're doing really well with the exercises if you've managed to complete them. You'll have learned which aspects of your character you're most proud of, which you'd like to change, and why. You'll have recalled some of the nuances of your younger self that made you happy and confident, and made an effort to recapture them within your current lifestyle. You'll have had a lateral look across the spectrum of your skills, both practical and emotional, and will have re-evaluated their usefulness in terms of your home and work life. You'll have challenged your current thinking and identified possible windows of new opportunity you may not have considered before. In short, you'll have been preparing to make adjustments that allow you to be the best 'you' possible for your future happiness.

Where to next?

The next chapter looks at the role that spirituality plays in all our lives, whether or not we're aware of it. Even if you regard yourself as a religious sceptic, you'll discover that spirituality is far wider reaching than the confines of any organized faith, and that life itself, in whatever form, is by its very nature spiritual. You'll have a chance to consider exploring different forms of spirituality, and teach yourself how to recognize spirituality at every turn in life. We'll also look at how giving – of yourself, your time, your possessions – can be one of the greatest bringers of happiness. Life isn't all about what we get out of it, but what we give back in at least equal part, and giving, in its many forms, can lead to powerful feelings of lasting joy.

My happiness journal

This space is for jotting down any thoughts, feelings or ideas you might have at this stage – it is purely optional.

→ **My thoughts on happiness at this moment**

_____

_____

_____

_____

_____

_____

_____

_____

_____

_____

_____

_____

_____

_____

_____

_____

_____

→ My ideas for change

_____

_____

_____

_____

_____

_____

_____

_____

_____

_____

_____

_____

_____

_____

_____

_____

_____

_____

_____

_____

_____

_____

_____

_____

10 *spirituality and the gift of giving*

'The spiritual path is simply the journey of living our lives. Everyone is on a spiritual path; most people just don't know it.'

Marianne Williamson, US spiritual activist, author and lecturer

Spirituality, to many people, means a belief in an organized religion or doctrine, but the reality is far broader than that. Some people define it as a feeling of connectedness to others and to nature; others describe it as a reflection on life's journey: less about the physical and more about the intangible. For those with a faith, belonging to a like-minded community can bring great comfort and strength, especially in tough times. It's not only the sense of being guided by a deity that worshippers hold dear, it's also the strong feeling that there is something more than mortal life, and that whatever trials they may face during this life, reward lies in the afterlife. Some people believe in a 'greater force' without acknowledging 'God'; others believe in God, but not in any particular faith.

Spiritualists who don't have faith may not adhere to any particular ideology, although some believe in cosmology – the influence of the Universe as a whole, lunar phases and the power of other forces such as the earth itself. Spirituality for others means introspection, enlightenment, reflection or a drive to promote simple, non-commercial living. If you've never thought of spirituality in these terms, perhaps it's time to re-evaluate your basic attitudes. If you spend time meditating, questioning your beliefs or contemplating the beliefs of others, this is a kind of spirituality. You might experience it as a feeling of being connected to the world and other people. You may find it through looking for a greater meaning or purpose to your own existence. Self-improvement can give rise to feelings of spirituality, especially if you devote any time to trying to make the quality of other people's lives better.

In a sense, whatever makes you deeply happy could be termed as spiritual: the enjoyment of a sunrise or sunset, for instance; or losing yourself in a piece of music; reading poetry or other insightful literature; enjoying physical closeness with a loved one; exploring your innermost feelings – all of these experiences can be described as spiritual.

For those who have faith, prayer can be a deeply spiritual experience – an outpouring of all that is in a person's heart, whether it's presented as contrition, thanksgiving, worship or supplication. Prayer can bring peace in the midst of inner conflict and induce feelings of joy. It can make the worshipper feel looked after and guided. For non-believers, contemplation is in itself a kind of prayer: an examination of the conscience; a resolve to try harder; a move towards self-forgiveness; a heartfelt longing for the world to be a better place.

Exercise 53

EXPLORE DIFFERENT FAITHS

In order to gain a deeper understanding of what different faiths have to offer, try to research one a week. You don't have to go in-depth: reading up on the internet or getting a basic book out of the library will give you an outline. You may decide on the strength of your reading that you want to visit a church, synagogue or mosque, for example, and experience a service for yourself. You may decide, on the other hand, that you've read enough to maintain whatever belief – or lack of belief – you have already. Either way, you'll have a greater insight into spirituality and a greater understanding of different groups of people by making yourself more familiar with faiths and their principles.

OTHER SPIRITUAL SOURCES

There are other sources of secular spirituality that some people use for guidance in their daily lives. Tarot, astrology, Kaballah, palmistry, clairvoyance, the healing power of reiki, self-hypnosis, meditation and visualization bring different levels of comfort to different people. Some individuals look to the predictions from Tarot card readings to help them make important and influential decisions in life; others turn to astrology and the alignment of the planets for answers to life's questions; palmistry and clairvoyance provide a similar 'guiding force' in some people's lives, although there's no scientific evidence to support the efficacy of any of these methods. The practices can bring comfort, but also disappointment if a wrong path is chosen or a prediction doesn't seem to come true, and relying heavily on these fatalistic methods may be inadvisable in the long term, especially as they tend to distance the individual from the responsibility for decisions made and actions taken.

Kaballah, although not an organized religion, considers itself a 'supplement' to conventional faiths. It's more a mystical journey, with followers practising meditation with a view to exploring their relationship with the *essence* of God, rather than God Himself. It's popular with celebrities and lay people alike, and was probably made most famous when Madonna started to embrace its principles.

Reiki is regarded by some to have a deeply spiritual aspect. It's a natural healing therapy that harnesses 'universal life energy', believed by advocates to be all around us, and which is practised by therapists who use themselves as a channel between this energy and the person they're treating. Its basis is that physical symptoms are manifestations of an imbalance of emotions, and that by rebalancing the soul, the body can be freed to heal itself. If you're interested in trying reiki, you can find a qualified practitioner near you by visiting the UK Reiki Federation website.

Self-hypnosis helps some people to get in touch with their innermost selves and sort out deep-seated fears, anxieties and issues with self-esteem. It's also been found to help with chronic pain in some individuals and is sometimes recommended by medical practitioners. Visualization is a similar technique that involves deep relaxation and creating images that are comforting and pleasurable to the individual. Both techniques are sometimes regarded as spiritual in nature because of the 'out-of-body' type of experience they can produce. Both should be taught by qualified practitioners.

Meditation and yoga are wonderful tools for relaxation and you can either teach yourself from books or online resources or, especially in the case of yoga, find a trained teacher. For meditation resources near you, visit www. metta.org.uk online, and you can find a qualified yoga teacher near you through The British Wheel of Yoga.

Exercise 54

BROADEN YOUR MIND

As in the *Explore different faiths* exercise earlier in the chapter, why not do some internet research into the practices described above? You'll gain more of an insight into whether or not any are for you, or if you might want

to have a taster by trying a session of one or more.
It's best to get word-of-mouth recommendations for
practitioners such as palmists, clairvoyants, Tarot readers
and astrologists, as there are no organizations to regulate
them. Reiki practitioners can be found via the UK Reiki
Federation and registered hypnotherapists through the
British Society of Clinical Hypnosis, although you should
always double-check a therapist's credentials before you
pay for their services.

→ # Emotional intelligence

*'It is not the strongest of the species that survives,
nor the most intelligent, but the one most
responsive to change.'*

Charles Darwin, English naturalist and author of *On the Origin of Species*

Emotional intelligence, often referred to as emotional
quotient (EQ), is thought by some researchers to be more
of a predictor of potential success and happiness than
intelligence quotient (IQ). Whilst IQ is a measure of a
person's intelligence quotient, EQ measures an individual's
ability to understand and act on their own emotions and to
empathize with others. Those with a high level of EQ are
able to assimilate the intelligence conferred by IQ and to
develop and organize knowledge efficiently, make measured
decisions and judgements, and communicate effectively.
Such strengths make for good leaders, team players and
networkers, all of which attributes are more likely to bring
personal fulfilment and happiness than IQ alone.

While some empirical studies seem to suggest that
individuals' IQ levels can be raised slightly, and that there
can be fluctuations in teenage years, there's little scientific
evidence to support this theory. Overall, scientists believe
that our IQ remains stable throughout life. It is possible, on

the other hand, to raise our EQ and make ourselves more confident, assertive and compassionate people. So how emotionally intelligent are you?

Exercise 55

TEST YOUR EQ

Consider the following statements and circle Yes or No.

→ I tend to let other people make decisions for me   Yes/No

→ I am generally indecisive   Yes/No

→ I tend to go with the flow rather than get what I want   Yes/No

→ I have a tendency to seek the approval of others   Yes/No

→ I don't like change   Yes/No

→ I find it hard to shake myself out of a bad mood   Yes/No

→ I am often irritable for no apparent reason   Yes/No

→ I feel generally dissatisfied with myself   Yes/No

→ I don't really like myself   Yes/No

→ I feel resentful that others don't
  understand me   Yes/No

→ I find it hard to communicate my wishes   Yes/No

→ I would describe myself as unassertive   Yes/No

→ I feel exploited in the workplace   Yes/No

→ I feel taken for granted by friends
  and/or family   Yes/No

→ I hardly ever keep my resolutions   Yes/No

→ I am envious of others' success   Yes/No

→ I get preoccupied with my own inadequacies   Yes/No

→ I would like to change but can never
  quite do it   Yes/No

→ I prefer not to talk about my emotions   Yes/No

→ I feel uncomfortable when others talk
  about their emotions   Yes/No

How many times did you answer 'Yes'?

0–5: Excellent EQ You're very in touch with your emotions and are aware of others' too. You instinctively know how to respond in a given emotional situation and could be a great organizer, team player, team leader and self-starter. You tend to have an optimistic take on life and have a go-getting personality. Others are drawn to you and trust your opinions and judgement. Keep it all going: you're a powerful motivator and a resilient individual. Your high EQ is a positive indicator of your potential for happiness.

6–10: High EQ You're doing well on the EQ front, managing life, taking the rough with the smooth and generally seeing the positive in given situations. You're a great listener and have a feel for when something is wrong in a relationship, whether personal or professional. You're not afraid to tackle issues head on, but could be a bit more assertive when it comes to your own needs and wishes. You could have a tendency to try to please others to the extent that you take a backseat to their wants. You can improve on this by repeating positive affirmations to yourself, along the lines of 'My needs are equally important'. See Chapter 3 for more on affirmations.

11–15: Moderate EQ You have a degree of EQ, but you're falling a bit short, which means you may experience more frustration than you need to. You'd like to put right the things that are wrong with your personal and work life, but need other people to motivate you to do so. You're slow to acknowledge your strengths and too ready to put yourself down, although you do recognize other people's strengths and vulnerabilities and can be a supportive person for them to turn to. Keep up this side of your nature and focus more on becoming a self-starter. Set yourself achievable goals, such as making an action plan for small changes, with deadlines to aim for. Reward yourself when you achieve any aim, however small, and feel good about yourself. Give your needs equal priority to those of others, too.

16–20: Low EQ You are lacking in self-esteem and self-confidence to the extent that you don't seem to matter much to yourself. Other people value you, and you value their opinions, so don't be afraid to ask them for a boost to your ego from time to time. Don't whinge and whine: just say 'I'm feeling a bit low. Remind me again of my strong points?', and try to keep it lighthearted. You can raise your own EQ by focusing on others, too. At the moment, you find it hard to connect on an emotional level, either with yourself or with others, and by recognizing other people's feelings and acting on them, you'll automatically make yourself feel valuable and good. Read up about assertiveness in Chapter 2 for more ideas on raising your self-esteem and, in turn, your EQ.

→ The gift of giving

'Since you get more joy out of giving joy to others, you should put a good deal of thought into the happiness that you are able to give.'

Eleanor Roosevelt, wife of Franklin Roosevelt, 32nd president of the USA

We are all spiritual beings if only through our creativity, imagination and connection with other people, and we can all benefit from moments of quiet reflection and from sometimes putting other people's needs before our own. The giving side of human nature is spiritual in itself.

When did you last give? It was probably earlier today and you were probably unaware that you were giving. Whether you spend five minutes listening to somebody; make someone a cup of tea without being asked; cook a meal for the family; pop a coin into a charity box or offer someone a lift, you're giving – and doesn't it feel good now you think about it? We can increase these positive feelings by focusing on giving, either materially or otherwise – not in order to receive praise or appreciation, but just to feel good about ourselves.

Perhaps you don't have a great deal of time to give to others, but any time devoted to another person is an act of kindness and generosity – the gift of giving; and giving generates love and respect, so there's every reason to try to give more. It's not about feeling sanctimonious or having an opportunity to boast to others about how lovely you are: it's about raising your own levels of self-esteem and self-worth. Giving yourself a pat on the back can feel as good as having someone else do it for you.

Exercise 56

COULD I GIVE MORE?

Have a think about whether you could be more giving, and therefore make yourself feel more worthwhile and, in turn, contented. Do you have elderly neighbours, for instance, who might appreciate the offer to pick up some groceries for them? Is there a local charity that might appreciate an hour or so spent distributing leaflets? Does your child's school need any parent helpers? Could you be a prison or hospital visitor? On a smaller scale, do you have any lonely relatives who would love a weekly phone call? Could you spend a little more time talking to your children about their school day or helping with homework? Is there a chore your partner detests that you could occasionally take on instead? Would they appreciate you running them a lovely, relaxing bath at the end of the day?

Now think how you feel when someone gives to you. Appreciated? Indebted? Grateful? Flattered? And how the giver feels? Generous? Kind? Selfless? Good? The feelings invoked by giving can be more rewarding and have greater resonance than those invoked by receiving.

In the space below, write down five things you could do to enable you to give more. It's not intended to be a pledge written in stone, just something to aim for. You'll feel the benefit as soon as you start giving a little more – and if it seems like a bit too much trouble, you'll feel even better for it.

I could...

1 _____

_____

_____

2 _____

_____

_____

3 _____

_____

_____

4 _____

_____

_____

5 _____

_____

_____

Summary

In this chapter you may have covered territory that was previously unknown to you: hopefully you'll have broadened your mind to the different possibilities that enjoying the spiritual side of life can bring. The very discovery and awareness of spirituality can bring a deep sense of peace to our lives, whether or not we have religious faith, and there is much to be explored that doesn't make up conventional faith, if you choose to pursue this path. You'll have discovered, too, how fulfilling giving of yourself can be, and that charity towards other people, whether material or otherwise, brings with it a heightened sense of self-esteem. The real reward for giving isn't in the thanks we receive, but the congratulations we can afford ourselves for taking the time and trouble and going that extra mile for the good of someone other than ourselves.

Where to next?

We are about to embark on the final chapter of the book now, and you'll have a chance to complete the self-evaluation questionnaire to discover your current happiness levels. Hopefully you'll have come some way towards happiness since you first picked the book up, and will find it useful to refer to as an ongoing guide. You'll find suggestions for exercises you can complete daily and less frequently to help you to revisit your happiness levels regularly. Then, if they start to slip, you can go back through the book and re-read sections and repeat exercises that most apply to you at that time.

My happiness journal

This space is for jotting down any thoughts, feelings or ideas you might have at this stage – it is purely optional.

→ **My thoughts on happiness at this moment**

_____

_____

_____

_____

_____

_____

_____

_____

_____

_____

_____

_____

_____

_____

_____

_____

_____

_____

_____

_____

→ My ideas for change

_____

_____

_____

_____

_____

_____

_____

_____

_____

_____

_____

_____

_____

_____

_____

_____

_____

_____

_____

_____

_____

_____

_____

_____

_____

_____

11 A re-evaluation

'*Happiness cannot come from without. It must come from within. It is not what we see and touch or that which others do for us which makes us happy; it is that which we think and feel and do, first for the other fellow and then for ourselves.*'

Helen Keller, deaf-blind American author, political activist and lecturer.

We are coming to the end of the workbook, and it's time to review the progress you have made to date. During the course of the chapters, we've worked together through long-held views you may have had about yourself, other people, matters of faith and spirituality, and how valid your beliefs about all these things have been over the years. Hopefully, we've managed to break down some of the reasons for the lack of personal happiness you were experiencing when you picked up this book, and to start to find ways to move forwards towards a deep and lasting contentment.

Through the various exercises, you'll have had a chance to look at life from a different viewpoint; to adjust your thinking – consciously, at first, then more instinctively. You'll have learnt that you can't please everyone all the time, and that your own opinion of yourself, your life choices and your achievements mean a great deal more in terms of self-fulfilment than what other people think of you. If you've been stuck in an unhappy situation – whether through a wrong career move; an unfulfilling relationship; a lack of self-care; getting bogged down by routine or being stuck in a rut of a different sort – you'll hopefully have been inspired to make some changes, bolstered by a new-found confidence, and with the knowledge that you can take your time as long as you are generally moving forward in a positive way.

If you've previously fallen into bad habits, such as over-eating, whether for comfort or through a lack of self-control; drinking too much and shunning exercise, hopefully you've become motivated to make achievable adjustments to your lifestyle so that, longer term, you'll gain not only fitness and better health, but a more positive view of yourself and your worth.

One of the lessons in this book is that there is so much reward to be gained for having given of ourselves a bit more than perhaps we're used to, and that the feeling of personal achievement that can be experienced through giving – especially with no thought of receiving anything in return – can bring intense feelings of contentment as well as gratitude for all that we already have.

Now, as promised, here again is the self-evaluation questionnaire you completed at the beginning of your journey. Take time to reflect on each statement before entering your answers, then see how far you've come.

Re-evaluation exercise

HOW HAPPY ARE YOU RIGHT NOW?

As at the beginning of the book, give each statement that's relevant to you a rating between 0–10, with 0 representing 'I completely disagree' and 10 representing

'I'm in total agreement'. Leave any statements that don't apply blank.

→ I feel generally happy with my lot _____

→ I make the most of every day _____

→ I find enough time just for me _____

→ I am fulfilled in my work _____

→ I feel appreciated in my work _____

→ My relationship is working well _____

→ I feel I'm a good enough partner _____

→ I find parenthood fulfilling and
  rewarding most of the time _____

→ I feel I'm a good enough parent _____

→ I have high self-esteem _____

→ Overall, I think I'm an optimist _____

→ I expect good things to happen to me _____

→ Good things usually do happen to me _____

→ I feel loved and supported by my
  family _____

→ I feel loved and supported by my
  friends _____

→ I have two or more close friends I can
  confide in   _____

→ I feel that people respect me   _____

→ I am spiritually fulfilled   _____

→ I like who I am   _____

→ I love my life!   _____

Add up your overall score, then find your average
mark out of ten by dividing this total by the number of
questions answered. This will give you your current overall
happiness rating. If your average is 7 or above, you're
well on your way to achieving greater happiness. If it's
less than 7, but greater than your score at the outset,
you're making progress and should congratulate yourself.
Re-read the chapters that have helped you most as you
continue on your journey, practise the exercises often
and take the re-evaluation questionnaire again in another
month or so's time. If your score hasn't improved from
when you first picked up the book, perhaps it would
benefit you to start again and really focus on the exercises
or, if you feel you may be depressed, to seek professional
help.

→ Moving on

Now that you've completed the workbook, that needn't be an
end to your quest for greater happiness. Self-improvement and
teaching yourself to be truly happy is an ongoing commitment,
and hopefully one that you are enjoying and gaining from
already. You can practise the exercises you've found most
helpful often – and the more you do, the more you'll find

yourself thinking more optimistically and behaving in a more positive way until it becomes close to second-nature. It's perfectly possible to teach yourself to be a more fulfilled, more rounded, sunnier and more joyful person and to spread the positivity around everyone you meet, so don't stop striving to be ever-more happy.

ONGOING EXERCISES

To help keep you on track, here's a checklist of exercises you should try to perform regularly. A quick glance at the list every day, to start with, will give you something to focus on. The book can remain your lifelong companion as time goes by if you check back now and then to refresh your memory and perhaps re-read relevant chapters. There are exercises to perform daily, weekly and sporadically, based on lessons you've already learned in earlier chapters.

Daily

Affirmations Repeat at least one positive affirmation ten times first thing in the morning. You can continue to do this throughout the day, changing the affirmation to strengthen your resolve in different areas. First thing on waking, for example, you could say 'Today will be a successful day for me'. Later, perhaps you'll choose something like 'Every hour I am achieving something good, however small'.

Blessings Before you go to sleep, focus on the positives in your life: your home, your family and friends, your rewarding job, your own self-improvement, your annual holiday – anything that brings you happiness on an ongoing basis.

'Me' time Treat yourself kindly and build some 'me' time into each day. It need only be 20 minutes if that's all you can manage, but spend it doing something indulgent but beneficial to your overall wellbeing.

Weekly

Set targets Not massive challenges, just small things that will make you feel good about yourself. You could aim to catch up with your emails, ring an old friend, sort out a cupboard or leave work on time more often.

Self-check At the end of each week – say on a Friday evening – review how many opportunities you've given yourself to feel relaxed and happy, rewarded or proud of yourself. Think back on how many compliments you've given or received, and make a note of any triumphs, no matter how small. Did you cook the perfect omelette? Stick to your new commitment to exercise? Achieve something noteworthy at work? Spend extra one-to-one time with the kids?

Ongoing

Set new goals We all like to coast along from time to time, given the opportunity, but striving to achieve bigger and better things is always a great way to keep motivated and bring purpose to our lives. If you've achieved the last set of goals you set for yourself, aim higher! If there are still things on your 'to do' wish list, for instance, have another look at how you might make them happen: maybe now is the time, when a previous occasion wouldn't have worked. Could you perhaps learn and master a new relaxation technique: self-hypnosis, Transcendental Meditation or visualization, for example?

Repeat the re-evaluation exercise To check your happiness levels, complete the re-evaluation questionnaire at intervals. If there are particular areas that are still not matching up to your expectations, work on these, using the relevant sections of the book. Keeping your social life fresh and interesting, connecting with more people from the past, or planning a more comfortable future, for instance, could all be things to aim for in order to achieve greater contentment.

'Here's to a happier, sunnier future!'

Taking it further

PUBLICATIONS AND RESEARCH PAPERS

Brodie, R. *Getting Past OK* (Hay House, 2003)

De Neve, Jan-Emmanuel. 'Functional polymorphism (5-HTTLPR) in the serotonin transporter gene is associated with subjective well-being: evidence from a US nationally representative sample' *Journal of Human Genetics*, 2011, 56, 456–9

Hadhazy, A. *Life's Extremes: Tightwads vs. Spendthrifts* (www.livescience.com)

Harris, R. *The Happiness Trap* (Robinson, 2008)

Moss, S. *Natural Childhood* (National Trust, 2012)

Plagnol, Anke C. and Easterlin, Richard A. 'Aspirations, Attainments, and Satisfaction: Life Cycle Differences Between American Women and Men' *Journal of Happiness Studies*, 2008, 9(4), 601–19

WEB RESOURCES

London School of Economics (LSE) www.lse.ac.uk

The National Trust www.nationaltrust.org.uk

University of Vienna http://psychologie.univie.ac.at/

www.brainyquote.com

www.thinkexist.com

ORGANIZATIONS

BeingAnOnly™
Tel: 020 8994 5964
www.beinganonly.com

Bill & Melinda Gates Foundation
www.gatesfoundation.org

The British Wheel of Yoga
Tel: 01529 306851
www.bwy.org.uk

Grant Thornton
www.grant-thornton.co.uk

The Laughter School
Tel: 01249 813 188; Mobile: 07836 796 215
www.thelaughterschool.com

Office for National Statistics
www.ons.gov.uk

Opinion Matters
Tel: 0207 251 9960
www.opinionmatters.co.uk

Personal Career Management
Tel: 0845 686 0745
www.personalcareermanagement.com

The UK Reiki Federation
Tel: 01264 791441
www.reikifed.co.uk

UNICEF
Tel: 0844 801 2414
www.unicef.org.uk

SELF-HELP FOR DEPRESSION

Depression Alliance
Tel: (Information pack request line) 0845 123 23 20
www.depressionalliance.org

Depression UK
www.depressionuk.org

SANE
Tel: (Helpline) 0845 767 8000
www.sane.org.uk

Index